The Apocalyptic Book of Isaiah

A New Translation with Interpretative Key

by
Avraham Gileadi

Hebraeus Press

Library of Congress cataloging data:

Gileadi, Avraham.
   The apocalyptic book of Isaiah: a new
translation with interpretative key. Provo,
Utah, Hebraeus Press. 208 p. 22 cm.

1. Bible. O. T. Isaiah. English. Gileadi, 1982.
2. Apocalyptic Literature. I. Title.
BS 1515.5   224.1   82-83040
ISBN 0-910511-00-4

Typographic design: Thomas K. Hinckley

Photolithographed by Community Press
Provo, Utah, United States of America

Preface

Why should I be writing this preface? I think it is because I have taught the rhetoric of Shakespeare and the Authorized Version for many years; and I find that the greatest difficulty readers have with older literature is that it is not concerned in the first place with logic or with chronological sequence. It demands that we ask questions like, Why do these two passages appear side by side? Why is something excluded that we might have expected to be in, and something else included that we should not have expected to be in? What are the repetitions of words and sounds for? Why is the same idea repeated more than once? And so on.

The Authorized Version of the Bible has the great advantage that it is the master of the older tradition of thinking and feeling about language; of all English translations, it became the basis of a number of Jewish and Christian versions. It no more bothers than the original did about what the logical or chronological sequence is: it follows the original in concentrating on more important things. For example, in 'Arise, shine; for thy light is come' (Isaiah 60.1), the repetition of the vowel gives the sense of a lift into unforgettable splendor.

At the same time, the language of the Authorized Version may be vague, either because the language was more loosely used in those days, or because the translators did not understand what they were translating, or because they felt that everything in the Hebrew had to be rendered in the English. Look at Isaiah 57.10: 'Thou art wearied in the greatness of thy way...Thou hast found the life of thine hand.' Gileadi has 'Though wearied by your excessive ways...You have found livelihood.' This is an ordinary sort of example that occurs many times. Now look at Isaiah 66.17: 'Eating swine's flesh, and the abomination, and the mouse.' Gileadi translates 'Who eat the flesh of swine and prawn and rodents.'

Here is an example where the wish of the translators to tie the chapter together by a series of 'fors' makes us try to find connections that are not there: Isaiah 55.8 has a 'for' that we can understand, because it follows on from verse 7. But the 'fors' in verses 9, 10, and 12 do not make the same connection. In verse 9, instead of 'For as the heavens are higher than the earth,' Gileadi has 'But as the heavens are higher than the earth.' In verse 10, instead of 'For as the rain cometh down' he has 'And,' and in verse 12 instead of 'For ye shall go out,' he has simply 'You shall depart.'

5

This may seem a slight example, but if we are reading at all carefully, the Authorized Version might make us puzzle over connections that are not there.

I have mentioned the older tradition of language. When the Lord is largely the author, and the message of the Most High is through his prophet, the nature of human authorship is secondary. In the same way, a *personal* style in the modern sense is irrelevant. The tradition of plain style in the scriptures (it was traditionally called *sermo humilis*, which means *humble* as well as *plain*) is never precious, never self-regarding, but not low—the plain style may be the highest style we know.

Yet the personality that does not put itself forward but allows itself to be a mouthpiece is indirectly very important. A committee making a translation has to agree. Half the committee may prefer A, half B; but they choose C because they can agree in compromise on C, although both A and B are better than C. One man, however, can, and should, decide for himself, as Tyndale did. With the tradition behind him, Dr. Gileadi has done this. In him come together qualifications which I believe have not been united before. As a qualified scholar in the Western sense, he takes advantage of modern scholarship without sharing in its disintegrative drive. His sense of *Isaiah* as a whole is more penetrating and detailed than any hitherto. His greater precision has reinforced the sense that *Isaiah* is a whole, not a number of passages stuck together.

In consequence, Dr. Gileadi has made a translation that is not simply an *aid* to the Authorized and other versions, but stands by itself, preserving the dignity and beauty of the Authorized Version, but with greater clarity, and more to the point, more concrete. As we read, we are not held up by incomprehension or puzzlement: we are able to understand more and therefore to feel more, not less; and the whole translation flows in a manner worthy of its supreme original.

Arthur Henry King

August, 1982

Contents

Foreword: Why a New Translation?

The Translating Process. The common method of biblical translation is to give a fixed form to a text which may be open to a wide variety of possible renderings. At best, this process consists of an inspired choice of words in the new language to express words and ideas already fixed by inspiration in the original language. This involves choosing one of perhaps half a dozen possible synonyms or synonymous expressions for a single word or expression in the biblical text. The effect of this choice is twofold. On the one hand, the translated scripture may be limited to only one meaning where perhaps two or more levels of meaning are intended in the original; on the other hand, the translated scripture may be plainer and less ambiguous than the biblical text precisely because of this limitation of the meaning. It should therefore be evident that a translated passage of scripture may not only be inferior to the biblical text because of possible mistranslation, but even when correctly translated may say less than the biblical text says. Thus the translator's task is to capture in the translation as much as possible the richness of meaning of the biblical text.

Early and Modern Translation. Since modern-English versions have become widely established among readers of the Bible, we can say, with gratifying hindsight, that a serious problem with the earlier versions is that their translations are frequently too literal. As in the translation of any literature, literalism can obscure or distort the sense of the original to the point where the reader feels uncomfortable with what is read. All this should go without saying. But one cannot on that account discredit the earlier versions, for each new generation of bible translations builds upon the work and experience of the former. From one generation of translations to the next, what is valid is generally retained and what is problematic discarded. Improvements in translation—in theory, not always in practice—are made on the basis of new knowledge that has accrued in the intervening period, whether as a result of the fever of biblical scholarship, such as has prevailed during the past 100 years, or the discovery of important new manuscripts and related linguistic and historical data. As is seen in the most recent generation of biblical versions, the main considerations in selecting one of several possible synonyms or synonymous expressions for a word or expression in the biblical text are the sense conveyed by the original and its colorful poetic imagery. It is now generally accepted that some flexibility of expression should be permitted the translator, or the translating process will lapse into literalism. But correct translation nevertheless remains strictly within the limits of the terms employed in the biblical text, unless, as on occasion, those terms are themselves in question.

The Various Bible Translations. The problem of literalism in biblical translation, and the resultant loss of meaning both to the translator and the reader, may best be demonstrated by comparing several passages from earlier versions to the New Translation of the Book of Isaiah:

Soncino Bible

10.23 For an extermination wholly
      determined
Shall the Lord, the God of hosts,
      make in the midst of all the earth.

New Translation

For my Lord, the Lord of Hosts,
      will carry out the utter destruction
      decreed upon the whole earth.

Douay Version

28.13 And the word of the Lord shall be
to them: Command, command again;
command, command again; expect,
expect again; expect, expect again:
a little there, a little there: that they
may go, and fall backward, and be
broken, and snared, and taken.

New Translation

So to them the word of the Lord
      remained:
Precept upon precept,
      precept upon precept,
measure by measure,
      measure by measure;
a trifle here, a trifle there,
      that, persisting,
they might lapse into stumbling
      and break themselves,
become ensnared
      and be taken captive.

King James Version

44.7 And who, as I, shall call, and shall
declare it, and set it in order for me,
since I appointed the ancient people?
and the things that are coming, and
shall come, let them shew unto them.

New Translation

Who predicts what happens as do I,
      and is the equal of me
in appointing a people from of old
      as types,
foretelling things to come?

Perhaps more objectionable than literalism in biblical translation is its opposite, liberalism. Factions of modern scholars, emancipated from the strictures of reverence for the biblical text and overconfident in their knowledge of philology and semantics, produced versions of the Bible whose renderings often obscure or distort even the most innocuous, undisputed passages of the text. Alternately, excessive reliance upon variant readings in ancient manuscripts whose authenticity is questionable has resulted in renderings that contradict both the tenor and context of individual passages. Examples of liberalism in biblical translation follow:

Living Bible	*New Translation*
14.3, 4 In that wonderful day when the Lord gives his people rest from sorrow and fear, from slavery and chains, you will jeer at the king of Babylon and say, "You bully, you! At last you have had what was coming to you!"	In the day the Lord gives you relief from grief and anguish, and from the arduous servitude imposed on you, you will take up this taunt against the king of Babylon, and say, How the tyrant has met his end and tyranny ceased!

Jerusalem Bible	*New Translation*
29.14 very well, I shall have to go on being prodigal of prodigious prodigies with this people. The wisdom of its sages shall decay, the intelligence of its intelligent men shall be shrouded.	therefore it is that I continue to astound these people with wonder upon wonder, rendering void the knowledge of their sages, the intelligence of their wise men insignificant.

New English Bible	*New Translation*
53.10 yet the Lord took thought for his tortured servant and healed him who had made himself a sacrifice for sin; so shall he enjoy long life and see his children's children, and in his hand the Lord's cause shall prosper.	But the Lord willed to crush him, causing him suffering, that, if he made his life an offering for guilt, he might see his offspring and prolong his days, and that the purposes of the Lord might prosper in his hand.

Exhibiting no grave problems of translation is the most recent generation of biblical versions, which seeks to steer a middle course between literalism and liberalism. Gone are the rigidity and archaisms of the past as well as the excesses of modern scholarship. In the Book of Isaiah, however, an important phenomenon has been overlooked even by modern conservative versions. As a result of literary studies outlined in the *Apocalyptic Key*, certain Isaianic terms whose primary function includes a description of the attributes of the Lord (viz., his *salvation,* his *righteousness,* his *wrath,* etc.) are seen to serve a secondary function as metaphors designating the chief characters that appear in the Book of Isaiah. In order of prominence, these are the Lord himself, a Davidic king, a Tyrant king, and the respective powers associated with each (see II,*b. An Entity Synthesis*). In other words, certain divine attributes appearing consistently throughout the Book of Isaiah are personified in the book's heroes and villains. Among non-Israelite nations of the ancient Near East, such a personification of divine attributes manifested itself in the plurality of gods of ancient Near Eastern mythology. As in so much of ancient Israelite practice, however, these mythical patterns are transformed in the Book of Isaiah to serve a literary purpose, namely, to conceal under pseudonyms, as in allegory, the actors in a great drama of the last days. This phenomenon is explained in greater detail in the *Apocalyptic Key*. It is necessary here merely to note that the use of certain metaphors, which include parts of the body (e.g., the Lord's *hand* and *voice*) and royal insignia (e.g., the Lord's *staff* and *ensign*), etc., requires that such terms in the Hebrew be translated literally and consistently in English. To my knowledge, no other translation of the Book of Isaiah, early or modern, achieves this, because scholars have not hitherto regarded the various sections of the Book of Isaiah as structurally interrelated. The following examples of inconsistencies in translation are taken from the most recent biblical versions (italics mine):

New American Bible	*New Translation*
13.2 Upon a bare mountain set up a signal; cry out to them, Wave for them to enter the gates of the volunteers.	Raise *the ensign* on a barren mountain; sound *the voice* among them! Beckon them with *the hand* to advance into the precincts of the elite.

Jewish Publication Society	_New Translation_
51.7 Listen to Me, you who care for the right, O people who lay My instruction to heart! Fear not the insults of men, And be not dismayed at their jeers;	Hear me, you who know _righteousness,_ O people in whose heart is my law: Do not fear the reproach of men; be undaunted by their ridicule.

New International Version	_New Translation_
62.11 The Lord has made proclamation to the ends of the earth: "Say to the Daughter of Zion, 'See, your Savior comes! See, his reward is with him, and his recompense accompanies him,' "	The Lord had made proclamation to the end of the earth: Tell the Daughter of Zion, See, your _Salvation_ comes, his reward with him, his work preceding him.

In summary, the New Translation, because it avoids both literalism and liberalism as well as inconsistencies in rendering certain key terms, may be considered prerequisite to a proper interpretation of the Book of Isaiah in English.

How to Use the New Translation. It is recommended that readers first read all or part of the New Translation of the Book of Isaiah to familiarize themselves with the text in its present rendering. A further reading of the text after study of the _Apocalyptic Key_ will then be more meaningful.

Words added to the text in order to clarify incomplete or difficult phrases appear in _italics_, unless they are implicit in the Hebrew.

Footnotes are generally self-explanatory. A problematic term or phrase in the text is marked by either a single italicized letter after it[a] or by two identical italicized letters, [b]one before and one after.[b]

Words or verses transposed from other parts of the text are set off by brackets [], but only at the point where they are relocated.

Abbreviations appearing in the footnotes include:

MT — The Masoretic Text, the Hebrew text from which the bulk of the New Translation is made

lQIsa[a]— The Dead Sea Scroll of Isaiah of St. Mark's Monastery, also in Hebrew

LXX — The (Greek) Septuagint Version

Heb. — Hebrew

1 The vision of Isaiah the son of Amoz which he beheld
concerning Judea and Jerusalem during the reigns of
Uzziah, Jotham, Ahaz, and Hezekiah, kings of Judah:

> 2 Hear, O heavens! Give heed, O earth!
>   The Lord has spoken:
> I have reared sons, brought them up,
>   but they have revolted against me.
> 3 The ox knows its owner,
>   the ass its master's stall,
> but Israel does not know;
>   my people are insensible.
> 4 Alas, a nation astray,
>   a people weighed down by sin,
> the offspring of wrongdoers,
>   perverse children:
> they have forsaken the Lord,
>   they have spurned the Holy One of Israel,
>   they have lapsed into apostasy.
>
> 5 Why be smitten further
>   by adding to your waywardness?
> The whole head is sick,
>   the whole heart diseased.
> 6 From the soles of the feet even to the head
>   there is nothing sound,
> only wounds and bruises and festering sores;
>   they have not been pressed out or bound up,
>   nor soothed with ointment.
>
> 7 Your land is ruined,
>   your cities burned with fire;
> your native soil is devoured by aliens
>   in your presence,
>   laid waste at its takeover by foreigners.
> 8 The Daughter of Zion is left
>   like a shelter in a vineyard,
> a hut in a melon field,
>   a city under siege.

9 Had not the Lord of Hosts left us
    a few survivors,
we should have been as Sodom,
    or become like Gomorrah.

10 Hear the word of the Lord,
    O leaders of Sodom;
give heed to the law of our God,
    you people of Gomorrah!
11 To what purpose are your abundant
    sacrifices to me? says the Lord.
I have had my fill of offerings of rams
    and fat of fatted beasts;
the blood of bulls and sheep and he-goats
    I do not want.
12 When you come to see me,
    who requires of you
    to trample my courts so?
13 Bring no more worthless offerings;
    they are as a loathsome incense to me.
As for convening meetings at the New Month
    and on the Sabbath,
wickedness with the solemn gathering
    I cannot approve.
14 Your monthly and regular meetings
    my soul detests.
They have become a burden on me;
    I am weary of putting up with them.
15 When you spread forth your hands,
    I will conceal my eyes from you;
though you pray at length,
    I will not hear:
    your hands are filled with blood.

16 Wash yourselves clean:
    remove your wicked deeds
from before my eyes;
    cease to do evil.

¹⁷ Learn to do good:
    demand justice,
    stand up for the oppressed;
  plead the cause of the fatherless,
    appeal on behalf of the widow.
¹⁸ Come now, let us put it to the test,
    says the Lord:
  though your sins are as scarlet,
    they can be made white as snow;
  though they have reddened as crimson,
    they may become *white* as wool.
¹⁹ If you are willing and obey,
    you shall eat the good of the land.
²⁰ But if you are unwilling and disobey,
    you shall be eaten by the sword.
  By his mouth the Lord has spoken it.

²¹ How the faithful city
    has become a harlot!
  She was filled with justice;
    righteousness made its abode in her,
    but now murderers.
²² Your silver has become dross,
    your wine diluted with water.
²³ Your rulers are renegades,
    accomplices of robbers:
  with one accord they love bribes
    and run after rewards;
  they do not dispense justice to the fatherless,
    nor does the widow's case come before them.

²⁴ Therefore the Lord, the Lord of Hosts,
    the Valiant One of Israel, declares,
  Woe to them! I will relieve me
    of my adversaries,
    avenge me of my enemies.
²⁵ I will restore my hand over you
    and smelt away your dross

as in a crucible,*a*
    and remove all your alloy.
²⁶ I will restore your judges as at the first,
    and your counsellors as in the beginning.
After this you shall be called
    the City of Righteousness,
    a faithful city.

²⁷ For Zion shall be ransomed by justice,
    those of her who repent by righteousness.
²⁸ But criminals and sinners
    shall be altogether shattered
when those who forsake the Lord
    are annihilated.
²⁹ And you*b* will be ashamed of the oaks
    you cherished
and blush for the parks
    you were fond of;
³⁰ you shall become like an oak
    whose leaves wither,
and as a garden
    that has no water.
³¹ The mighty shall be as refuse,
    and their works a spark;
both shall burn up alike,
    and there shall be none to extinguish.

2   A prophecy concerning Judea and Jerusalem which
    Isaiah the son of Amoz saw in vision:

    ² In the latter days
        the mountain of the Lord's house
    shall become established
        as*a* the head of the mountains;

---

a25 Heb. *kabbōr, as with potash/lye,* emended to *kakūr;* cf. 48.10
b29 Heb. *they*
a2   So 1QIsaᵃ; MT has *bet essentiae: in/as*

> it shall be preeminent among the hills,
>> and all nations will flow to it.
> ³ Many peoples shall go, saying,
>> Come, let us go up
> to the mountain of the Lord,
>> to the house of the God of Jacob,
> that he may instruct us in his ways,
>> that we may follow in his paths.
> For out of Zion shall go forth the law,
>> and from Jerusalem the word of the Lord.
> ⁴ He will judge between the nations
>> and arbitrate for many peoples.
> They will beat their swords into plowshares,
>> their spears into pruning hooks:
> nation will not lift the sword against nation,
>> nor will they learn warfare any more.

> ⁵ O house of Jacob, come,
>> let us follow the light of the Lord.

> ⁶ For thou, *O Lord*, hast forsaken thy people,
>> the house of Jacob, because,
> like the Philistines,
>> they provide themselves with^{*b*}
> mystics from the East
>> and are content with the infantile heathen.
> ⁷ Their land is full of silver and gold
>> and there is no end to their wealth;
> their land is full of horses
>> and there is no end to their chariots.
> ⁸ Their land is full of idols:
>> they adore the works of their hands,
>> things their own fingers have made.
> ⁹ Mankind is brought low
>> when men thus debase themselves.
> Forbear them not!

---

*b*6   Heb. conjunctive *wĕ* emended to preposition *bĕ*

18

¹⁰ Go into the rocks;
    hide in the dust
  from the awesome presence of the Lord
    and from the brightness of his glory.
¹¹ The haughty eyes of men shall be lowered
    and man's pride abased;
  the Lord alone shall be exalted
    in that day.

¹² The Lord of Hosts has a day in store
    for all the proud and arrogant
  and for all who are exalted,
    that they may be brought low.
¹³ *It shall come* against all the lofty
    cedars of Lebanon
  that lift themselves up high,
    and against all the oaks of Bashan,
¹⁴ against all high mountains
    and elevated hills,
¹⁵ against every tall tower
    and reinforced wall,
¹⁶ against [all vessels at sea,]*c*
    both merchant ships*d* and pleasure craft.
¹⁷ The haughtiness of men shall be abased,
    and man's pride brought low;
  the Lord alone shall be exalted
    in that day.

¹⁸ He will utterly supplant the false gods.

¹⁹ Men will go into caves in the rocks
    and holes in the ground,
  from the awesome presence of the Lord
    and from the brightness of his glory,
    when he arises and strikes terror on earth.
²⁰ In that day men will throw away
    to the moles and to the bats

*c*16   So LXX; line does not appear in MT
*d*16   Heb. *ships of Tarshish*

their idols of silver and gods of gold
  which they have made for themselves
  to adore.
²¹ Men will go into crevices in the rocks
  and fissures in the cliffs,
from the awesome presence of the Lord
  and from the brightness of his glory,
  when he arises and strikes terror on earth.
²² Desist from the things of man,
  in whose nostrils is but breath!
For of what consideration is he?

3
Even now, the Lord, the Lord of Hosts,
  deprives Judea and Jerusalem
of both staff and crutch—
  of all food supply and water supply,
² of the valiant man and soldier,
  the magistrate and prophet,
  the augur and elder,
³ the officer and dignitary,
  advisers, skilled craftsmen, and rhetoricians.
⁴ I, *the Lord,* will make adolescents their rulers;
  delinquents will lord it over them.
⁵ People will oppress one another,
  every man his neighbor.
The young will be insolent to the elderly,
  the vile to the honorable.

⁶ Then will a man apprehend a kinsman
  of his father's house, *and say,*
You have a tunic: be our leader,
  and take charge of this ruination!
⁷ But he will raise *his hand* in that day
  and swear, I am no physician.
There is neither food nor clothing in my house;
  you cannot make me a leader of the people.

⁸ Jerusalem will falter and Judea fall,
   because their tongue and their actions
are contrary to the Lord,
   an affront to his glory before his very eyes.
⁹ The look on their faces betrays them:
   they flaunt their sin like Sodom;
   they cannot hide it.
Woe to their souls;
   they have brought disaster upon themselves!

¹⁰ Tell the righteous it shall be well with them;
   they shall eat the fruits of their own labors.
¹¹ But woe to the wicked
   when calamity *overtakes them*:
they shall be paid back
   for the deeds they have done!

¹² As for my people, babes subject them;
   women wield authority over them.
O my people, your leaders mislead you,
   abolishing your traditional ways.
¹³ The Lord will take a stand
   and contend with them;
   he has arisen to judge the nations.
¹⁴ He will bring to trial the elders of his people
   and their rulers, *and say to them,*
It is you who have devoured the vineyard;
   you fill your houses by depriving the needy.
¹⁵ What do you mean by oppressing my people,
   humbling the faces of the poor?
says the Lord of Hosts.

¹⁶ The Lord says, moreover,
   Because the women of Zion are haughty
and put on airs,
   painting their eyes,
ever flirting when they walk,
   and clacking with their feet,

> [17] the Lord will afflict the scalps
>> of the women of Zion with baldness;
>> the Lord will expose their private parts.

[18] In that day the Lord will strip away their finery—the anklets, head ornaments and crescents, [19] the pendants, chains and scarves, [20] tiaras, bracelets and ribbons, zodiac signs and charm amulets, [21] rings for the fingers and for the ears, [22] the elegant dress, the shawl, the kerchief and the purse, [23] hosiery, sheer linen, millinery and cloaks.

> [24] And instead of perfume there shall be a stench,
>> instead of the girdle, a piece of twine,
> instead of the coiffure, baldness,
>> instead of the festive dress,
>> a loincloth of burlap;
> for in place of beauty
>> there shall be ignominy.[a]
> [25] Your men shall be felled by the sword,
>> your might *overthrown* in war.
> [26] Her gateways shall lie bereaved and forlorn;
>> she shall sit on the ground destitute.

4   Seven women will take hold of one man
>> in that day, and say,
> We will eat our own food,
>> wear our own clothes,
> only let us be called by your name—
>> take away our reproach!

[2] In that day the plant of the Lord shall be beautiful and glorious, and the earth's fruit the pride and glory of the survivors of Israel. [3] Then shall they who are left in Zion and they who remain in Jerusalem be called holy—all who were inscribed to be among the living at Jerusalem. [4] *This shall be* when my Lord has washed away the excrement of the women of Zion and cleansed Jerusalem of its bloodshed,

---

a24   So 1QIsaᵃ; term does not appear in MT

in the spirit of justice, by a burning wind. ⁵ Over the whole
site of Mount Zion, and over its solemn assembly, the Lord
will form a cloud by day and a mist glowing with fire by
night: above all that is glorious shall be a canopy. ⁶ It shall
be a shelter and shade from the heat of the day, a secret
refuge from the downpour and from rain.

5

Let me sing for my beloved
    a love song about his vineyard:
My beloved had a vineyard
    on the fertile brow of a hill.
² He cultivated it, clearing it of stones,
    and planted it with choice vines.
He built a watchtower in its midst
    and hewed for it a winepress as well.
Then he expected it to yield grapes,
    but it produced wild grapes.

³ Now, O inhabitants of Jerusalem
    and you men of Judea,
    please judge between me and my vineyard!
⁴ What more could have been done
    for my vineyard than I have done for it?
When I expected it to yield grapes,
    why did it produce wild grapes?
⁵ Let me now inform you
    what I will do to my vineyard:
I will have its hedge removed
    and let it be burned;
I will have its wall broken through
    and let it be trampled.
⁶ I will make it a desolation:
    it shall be neither pruned nor hoed,
    but briars and thorns shall overgrow it.
Moreover, I will forbid the rainclouds
    to rain on it.
⁷ The vineyard of the Lord of Hosts
    is the house of Israel

and the men of Judah
his cherished grove.
He expected justice,
but there was injustice;
he expected righteousness,
but there was an outcry.

⁸ Woe to those who join house to house
and link field to field till no place is left,
and you are restricted to dwell
in the centers of the land!
⁹ The Lord of Hosts *spoke this* in my hearing:
Surely many buildings shall lie desolate,
large and fine *houses* unoccupied.
¹⁰ A ten-acre*ᵃ* vineyard shall yield but one bath,*ᵇ*
a homer*ᶜ* of seed but an ephah.*ᵈ*

¹¹ Woe to those who go after liquor
as soon as they arise in the morning,
who linger at night parties,
inflamed by wine!
¹² There are harps and lyres,
drums, flutes and wine at their banquets,
but they regard not what the Lord does,
nor perceive his hands at work.
¹³ Therefore are my people exiled
without knowing why;
their best men die of famine,
their masses perish with thirst.
¹⁴ Sheol becomes ravenous,
opening its mouth insatiably;
into it descend their elite with the masses,
their boisterous ones and revelers.

*a*10   Heb. *ten-yoke*, viz., the land plowed by ten yoke of oxen in one day
*b*10   About 6 gallons or 22 liters
*c*10   About 6 bushels or 220 liters
*d*10   A tenth of a homer

¹⁵ Mankind is brought low
    when men debase themselves,
  causing the eyes of the high-minded
    to be downcast.
¹⁶ But the Lord of Hosts will be exalted
    by a just judgment,
  the holy God show himself holy
    by *his* righteousness.
¹⁷ Then shall *his* sheep feed in their pasture
    and proselytes eat in the ruins of the affluent.

¹⁸ Woe to those drawn to sin by vain attachments,
    hitched to transgression like a trailer,
¹⁹ who think, Let him quickly speed up his work
    so we may see it!
  Let the plan of the Holy One of Israel
    soon come to pass,
    and we will know!

²⁰ Woe to those who suppose
    what is evil to be good
    and what is good, evil!
  They put darkness for light
    and light for darkness;
  they make bitterness sweet
    and the sweet bitter.

²¹ Woe to those who are wise in their own eyes
    and clever in their own view!

²² Woe to those who are valiant at drinking wine
    and champions at mixing liquor!

²³ *Woe to those* who acquit the guilty for a bribe,
    but deny justice to the innocent!
²⁴ As a blazing fire consumes stubble
    and as dry weeds wane before the flame,
  so shall their roots decay away
    and their blossoms fly up like dust.

For they have despised the law
of the Lord of Hosts
and reviled the words
of the Holy One of Israel.
²⁵ Therefore the anger of the Lord is kindled
against his people:
he draws back his hand against them
and strikes them;
the mountains quake, and their corpses
lie like litter about the streets.

Yet for all this his anger is not abated;
his hand is upraised still.

²⁶ He raises an ensign to distant nations
and summons them from beyond the horizon.
Forthwith they come,
swiftly and speedily.
²⁷ Not one of them grows weary,
nor does any waver;
they do not drowse or fall asleep.
Their waist-belts come not loose
nor their sandal thongs undone.
²⁸ Their arrows are sharp;
all their bows are strung.
The tread of their warhorses resembles flint;
their chariot wheels revolve like a whirlwind.
²⁹ They have the roar of a lion;
they are aroused like young lions:
growling, they seize the prey, and escape,
and none comes to the rescue.
³⁰ He shall be stirred up against them in that day,
even as the Sea is stirred up.
And should one look to the land,
there *too* shall be a distressing gloom,
for the daylight shall be darkened
by an overhanging mist.

6 In the year of king Uzziah's death, I saw my Lord seated on a throne, highly exalted, the skirt of his robe filling the sanctuary. ²Seraphs stood by him overhead, each having six wings—with two they could veil their presence, with two conceal their location, and with two fly about. ³They called out to one another, and said,

Most holy is the Lord of Hosts;

the consummation of the whole earth is his glory!
⁴The threshold shook to its foundation at the sound of those who called, and a mist filled the temple.
⁵Then I thought, Woe is me: I have been struck dumb, for I am a man of unclean speech, and I live among a people of unclean speech: I have seen the King, the Lord of Hosts, with my own eyes!
⁶Then one of the seraphs flew to me carrying an ember which he had taken with tongs from the altar. ⁷Touching it to my mouth, he said, See, this has touched your lips: your sins are taken away, your transgressions atoned for.
⁸Then I heard the voice of my Lord saying, Whom shall I send? Who will go for us? And I replied, Here am I; send me.
⁹And he said, Go, and say to these people,

Go on hearing, but not understanding;

Go on seeing, but not perceiving.

¹⁰Make the heart of these people grow fat;

dull their ears

and shut their eyes,

lest they see with their eyes

and hear with their ears,

understand in their heart,

and repent and be healed.
¹¹And I replied, For how long, my Lord? And he said,

Until the cities lie desolate

and without inhabitant,

the houses without a man,

and the land ravaged to ruin.

¹² For the Lord will drive men away,
and great shall be the exodus
from the centers of the land.
¹³ And while yet a tenth *of the people*
remain in it, or return,
they shall be burned.
But like the terebinth or the oak
when it is felled,
whose stump remains alive,
so shall the holy offspring
be what is left standing.

7 When Ahaz son of Jotham, the son of Uzziah, was
king of Judah, Rezin king of Aram and Pekah son of
Remaliah king of Israel came up to Jerusalem to wage war
against it, but could not overpower it.
² And when the house of David was informed that Aram
was leading Ephraim on, the king's mind and the minds of
his people were shaken, as trees in a forest are shaken by
a gale.
³ Then the Lord said to Isaiah, Go out and meet Ahaz, you
and your son Shear-Jashub,^a at the end of the aqueduct of
the Upper Reservoir, on the road to the Laundry Plaza.
⁴ Say to him, See to it that you remain calm and unafraid.
Be not intimidated by these two smoking tail ends of kind-
ling, by the burning anger of Rezin and Aram and the son
of Remaliah, ⁵ even though Aram has conceived an evil
plot against you, as has Ephraim and the son of Remaliah,
who say, ⁶ Let us invade Judah and stir up trouble there.
We will take it for ourselves by force and set a ruler over
it—the son of Tabeal.
⁷ Thus says my Lord the Lord:
It shall not occur
or transpire.
⁸ For as surely as Damascus
is the capital of Aram

a3   I.e., *A remnant will return*

28

and Rezin the head of Damascus,
within sixty-five years shall Ephraim
be shattered as a nation.
⁹But as surely as Samaria
is the capital of Ephraim
and the son of Remaliah
the head of Samaria,
you will not believe it,
because you are not loyal.

¹⁰Again the Lord addressed Ahaz, and said, ¹¹Ask a sign
for yourself from the Lord your God, whether in the depths
below or in the heights above. ¹²But Ahaz said, I will not.
I will not put the Lord to the test.

¹³Then *Isaiah* said, Take heed, O house of David! Is it not
enough for you to try the patience of men? Must you also
try the patience of my God?

¹⁴Therefore will my Lord of himself give you a sign: the
young woman with child shall give birth to a son and
name him Immanuel.*ᵇ* ¹⁵Cream and honey will he eat by
the time he has learned to reject what is evil and choose
what is good. ¹⁶But before the child learns to reject the
evil and choose the good, the land whose two rulers you
loathe shall lie forsaken. ¹⁷The Lord will bring upon you
and your people and your father's house a day unlike any
since Ephraim broke away from Judah—*the day of* the king
of Assyria.

¹⁸In that day the Lord will signal for the flies from the far
rivers of Egypt and for the bees in the land of Assyria.

¹⁹And they will come and settle with one accord in the
riverbeds of the prairie and in rocky ravines, and by all
ditches and water holes. ²⁰In that day my Lord will use a
razor hired at the River—the king of Assyria—to shave
your head and the hair of your legs, and to cut off even
your beard.

²¹In that day a man will keep alive a young cow and a
pair of sheep. ²²And because of their plentiful milk, men

*b*14   I.e., *God is with us*

will eat the cream. All who remain in the land will feed on cream and honey.

²³ In that day every plot of ground with a thousand vines worth a thousand pieces of currency shall be briars and thorns. ²⁴ Men will go there with bows and arrows, for the whole land shall revert to wilderness. ²⁵ And on all hillsides cultivated by the hoe you will no longer go for fear of the briars and thorns, but they shall serve as a cattle range, a terrain for sheep to tread down.

8 The Lord said to me, Take a large scroll and write on it in common script: Hasten the plunder, hurry the spoil. ² And I called in reliable witnesses, Uriah the priest and Zechariah the son of Jeberechiah, to witness for me.

³ And when I had been with the prophetess, she conceived and gave birth to a son. And the Lord said to me, Name him Maher-Shalal-Hash-Baz.ᵃ ⁴ For before the child knows how to say, Father, or Mother, the wealth of Damascus and the plunder of Samaria will be brought before the king of Assyria.

⁵ The Lord addressed me again, and said,
> ⁶ Because these people have rejected
>   the waters of Shiloah, which flow gently,
>   and rejoice in Rezin
>   and the son of Remaliah,
> ⁷ therefore will my Lord
>   cause to come up over them
>   the great and mighty waters of the River—
>   the king of Assyria in all his glory.
>   He will rise up over all his channels
>   and overflow all his banks.
> ⁸ He will sweep into Judea *like* a flood
>   and, passing through, reach the very neck;
>   his outspread wings will span
>   the breadth of your land, O Immanuel.

*a*3   I.e., *Hasten the plunder, hurry the spoil*

⁹Though nations form pacts,
 they shall be routed.
 Give heed, all you distant lands!
You may take courage in one another,
 but shall be in fear;
you may arm yourselves,
 but shall be terrorized.
¹⁰Though you hold consultations,
 they shall come to nought;
though you make proposals,
 they shall not prove firm:
God is with us!

¹¹The Lord spoke to me, clasping my hand, and admonished me not to follow the ways of these people. For he said,
 ¹²Do not call a conspiracy all that these people
  call a conspiracy;
 be not afraid or awed
  by the thing they fear.
¹³But sanctify the Lord of Hosts,
 making him your fear, him your awe.
¹⁴And *to you* he will be a sanctuary,
 but to the two houses of Israel
a stumbling block or obstructing rock,
 and a snare, catching unawares
 the inhabitants of Jerusalem.
¹⁵Many will stumble into them,
 and when they fall shall be broken,
and when they become ensnared
 shall be taken captive.

¹⁶*For the Lord has said,*
 Bind up the testimony;
 seal the law among my disciples.
¹⁷I will wait for the Lord,
 who hides his face from the house of Jacob,
 and expect him.

¹⁸ As for me and the children the Lord has given me, we shall be signs and portents in Israel from the Lord of Hosts, who dwells in Mount Zion.

¹⁹When men tell you to inquire of mediums and spiritists who huddle together and mutter, *say to them,* Should not a people inquire of their God? Should one inquire*ᵇ* of the dead on behalf of the living ²⁰for doctrine and for a testimony? Surely, while they utter such words devoid of light, ²¹they roam about embittered by hunger; and when they are hungry, they become enraged and, gazing upward, curse their king and their God. ²²They will look to the land, but there shall be a depressing scene of anguish and gloom; and thus are they banished into outer darkness.

9 But it shall not be gloomy to those who have been in anguish for her. In the past he humbled the land of Zebulon and Naphtali, but at the last he will exalt the sea route by the Jordan *in* Galilee of the nations.

> ²The people walking in darkness
>   have seen a bright light;
>   on the inhabitants of the land
>   of the shadow of death
>   has the light dawned.
> ³Thou hast enlarged the nation
>   and increased its joy;
>   they rejoice at thy presence
>   as men rejoice at harvest time,
>   or as men are joyous when they divide spoil.
> ⁴For thou hast smashed the yoke
>   that burdened them,
>   the staff of submission,
>   the rod of those who subjected them,
>   as in the day of Midian*'s defeat.*
> ⁵And all boots used in battle
>   and tunics rolled in blood
>   have become fuel for bonfires.

*b*19   So LXX; phrase lacking in MT

⁶For to us a child is born, a son appointed,
    who will shoulder the burden of government.
He will be acclaimed
    Wonderful Counsellor, Mighty in Valor,
    a Father for Ever, a Prince of Peace,
⁷that sovereignty may be extended
    and peace have no end;
that, on the throne of David
    and over his kingdom,
his rule may be established and upheld
    by justice and righteousness
    from this time forth and forever.
The zeal of the Lord of Hosts will accomplish it.

⁸This message my Lord sent to Jacob,
    and it shall befall Israel.
⁹And the entire people—
    Ephraim and those who dwell in Samaria—
shall know of it,
    who say in pride and arrogance of heart,
¹⁰The bricks have fallen down,
    but we will rebuild with hewn stone;
the sycamores have been felled,
    but we will replace them with cedars!
¹¹But the Lord will strengthen
    Rezin's enemies against them
    when he stirs up their adversaries:
¹²Aramaeans from the east
    and Philistines from the west
    will devour Israel with open mouth.

Yet for all this his anger is not abated;
    his hand is upraised still.

¹³But the people do not turn back
    to him who smites them,
nor will they inquire
    of the Lord of Hosts.

¹⁴ Therefore the Lord will cut off from Israel
    head and tail, palm top and reed,
    in a single day;
¹⁵ the elders or notables are the head,
    the prophets who teach falsehoods the tail.
¹⁶ The leaders of these people have misled them,
    and those who are led are confused.
¹⁷ My Lord is not pleased with their young men,
    nor does he pity their fatherless and widows,
because all alike are godless malefactors,
    and every mouth utters profanities.

Yet for all this his anger is not abated;
    his hand is upraised still.

¹⁸ Wickedness shall be set ablaze like a fire,
    and briars and thorns shall it consume;
it shall ignite the jungle forests,
    and they shall billow upward
    in mushrooming clouds of smoke.
¹⁹ At the wrath of the Lord of Hosts
    the earth is scorched,
    and people are but fuel for the fire.
Men will have no compassion
    one for another.
²⁰ They will snatch on the right,
    yet remain hungry;
they will devour on the left,
    but not be satisfied:
men will eat the flesh
    of their own offspring.
²¹ Manasseh *will turn* against Ephraim
    and Ephraim against Manasseh,
and both will combine against Judah.

Yet for all this his anger is not abated;
    his hand is upraised still.

10 Woe to those who enact unjust laws,
   who draft oppressive legislation—
²denying justice to the needy,
   depriving the poor of my people of their rights,
making plunder of widows,
   mere spoil of the fatherless!
³What will you do in the day of reckoning,
   when the holocaust overtakes you from afar?
To whom will you flee for help?
   Where will you leave your wealth?
⁴There shall nothing remain
   but to kneel among the captives
   or fall among the slain.

Yet for all this his anger is not abated;
   his hand is upraised still.

⁵Hail the Assyrian, the rod of my anger!
   My wrath is a staff in his hand.
⁶I will commission him against a godless nation,
   appoint him over the people
   deserving of my vengeance,
to pillage for plunder, to spoliate for spoil,
   to tread underfoot like mud in the streets.
⁷Nevertheless, it shall not seem so to him;
   this shall not be what he has in mind.
His purpose shall be to annihilate
   and to exterminate nations not a few.
⁸**He will say, Are not my commanders kings,**
   one and all?
⁹Has not Calno fared like Carchemish?
   Is not Hamath as Arpad,
   Samaria no better than Damascus?
¹⁰Since I could do this to the pagan states,
   whose statues exceeded
   those of Jerusalem and Samaria,
¹¹shall I not do to Jerusalem and its images
   even as I did to Samaria and its idols?

¹²But when my Lord has fully accomplished his work in Mount Zion and in Jerusalem, he will punish the king of Assyria for his notorious boasting and infamous conceit, ¹³because he said,

> I have done it by my own ability
>> and shrewdness, for I am ingenious.
> I have done away with the borders of nations,
>> I have ravaged their reserves,
>> I have vastly reduced the inhabitants.
> ¹⁴I have impounded the wealth of peoples
>> like a nest,
> and I have gathered up the whole world
>> as one gathers abandoned eggs;
> not one flapped its wings,
>> or opened its mouth to utter a peep.

> ¹⁵Shall an axe exalt itself
>> above the one who hews with it,
> or a saw vaunt itself
>> over him who handles it?
> As though the rod wielded him who lifts it up!
>> As though the staff held up the one
>> who is not made of wood!
> ¹⁶Therefore will the Lord, the Lord of Hosts,
>> send a consumption into his fertile lands
> and cause a fire to flare up
>> like a burning hearth,
>> to undermine his glory:
> ¹⁷the Light of Israel will be the fire
>> and their Holy One the flame,
> and it shall burn up and devour
>> his briars and thorns in a single day.
> ¹⁸His choice forests and productive fields
>> it will consume, both life and substance,
>> turning them into a rotting morass.
> ¹⁹And the trees left of his forest shall be so few,
>> a child could record them.

²⁰ In that day those who survive of Israel
and who escape of the house of Jacob
will no longer rely on him who struck them,
but will truly rely on the Lord,
the Holy One of Israel:
²¹ of Jacob a remnant will return
to the one Mighty in Valor.
²² For though your people, O Israel,
be as the sands of the sea,
only a remnant will return;
although annihilation is decreed,
it shall overflow with righteousness.
²³ For my Lord, the Lord of Hosts,
will carry out the utter destruction
decreed upon the whole earth.

²⁴ Therefore, thus says my Lord,
the Lord of Hosts:
O my people who inhabit Zion,
be not afraid of the Assyrians,
though they strike you with the rod
or raise their staff over you,
as did the Egyptians.
²⁵ For my anger will very soon come to an end;
my wrath will become their undoing.
²⁶ The Lord of Hosts will raise the whip
against them,
as when he struck the Midianites
at the rock of Oreb.
His staff is over the Sea,
and he will lift it over them,
as he did to the Egyptians.
²⁷ In that day their burdens shall be lifted
from your shoulders,
their yoke *removed* from your neck:
the yoke *that wore away your fatness*
shall by fatness wear away.

²⁸ He advances on Aiath, passes through Migron;
    at Micmash he marshals his weaponry.
²⁹ They cross over the pass,
    stopping overnight at Geba.
  Ramah is in a state of alarm,
    Gibeah of Saul is fleeing.
³⁰ Cry out, O Daughter of Gallim!
    Hear her, Laishah; answer her, Anathoth!
³¹ Madmenah has moved out of the way,
    the inhabitants of Gebim are in full flight.
³² This same day he will but pause at Nob
    and signal the advance
  against the mountain of the Daughter of Zion,
    the hill of Jerusalem.
³³ Then will the Lord, the Lord of Hosts,
    shatter the towering *trees*
    with terrifying power;
  the high in stature shall be hewn down,
    the lofty ones leveled.
³⁴ The dense forests shall be battered down
    with *the force of* iron,
    and Lebanon fall spectacularly.

11
A shoot will spring up from the stock of Jesse
    and a branch from its base bear fruit.
² The Spirit of the Lord will rest upon him—
    the spirit of wisdom and of understanding,
  the spirit of counsel and of valor,
    the spirit of knowledge
    and of the fear of the Lord.
³ His intuition will be *guided*
    by the fear of the Lord;
  he will not judge by what his eyes see,
    nor establish proof by what his ears hear.
⁴ He will judge the poor with righteousness,
    and with equity arbitrate
    for the lowly in the land;

he will smite the earth
　　with the rod of his mouth
and with the breath of his lips
　　slay the wicked.
⁵ Righteousness will be as a band about his waist,
　　faithfulness a girdle round his loins.

⁶ Then shall the wolf dwell among lambs
　　and the leopard lie down with young goats;
calves and young lions *will feed*[a] together,
　　and a youngster will lead them *to pasture*.
⁷ When a cow and bear browse,
　　their young will rest together;
　　the lion will eat straw like the ox.
⁸ A suckling infant will play near the adder's den,
　　and the toddler reach his hand
　　over the viper's nest.
⁹ There shall be no harm or injury done
　　throughout my holy mountain,
for the earth shall be filled
　　with the knowledge of the Lord
　　as the oceans are overspread with waters.

¹⁰ In that day the sprig of Jesse,
　　who stands for an ensign to the peoples,
shall be sought by the nations,
　　and his residence shall be glorious.
¹¹ In that day my Lord will again *raise*[b] his hand
　　to reclaim the remnant of his people—
those who shall be left out of Assyria,
　　Egypt, Pathros, Cush, Elam, Shinar, Hamath
　　and the islands of the sea.
¹² He will raise the ensign to the nations
　　and assemble the exiled of Israel;
he will gather the scattered of Judah
　　from the four directions of the earth.

*a*6　So 1QIsaᵃ; LXX. MT reads *and fatlings*
*b*11　Heb. *šēnît, a second time,* emended to *śĕʾēt;* cf. Scott, *IB,* 5, p. 251

39

¹³ Ephraim's jealousy shall pass away
and the hostile ones of Judah be cut off;
Ephraim will not envy Judah,
nor Judah resent Ephraim.

¹⁴ But they will swoop on the Philistine flank
toward the west,
and together plunder those to the east;
they will take Edom and Moab at hand's reach,
and the Ammonites will obey them.

¹⁵ The Lord will dry up the tongue
of the Egyptian Sea ^cby his mighty wind;^c
he will extend his hand over the River
and smite it into seven streams
to provide a way on foot.

¹⁶ And there shall be a pathway out of Assyria
for the remnant of his people
who shall be left,
as there was for Israel
when it came up from the land of Egypt.

12

In that day you will say,
I praise thee, O Lord.
Although thou hast been angry with me,
thine anger is turned away
and thou hast consoled me.

² In^a the God of my salvation I will trust
without fear;
for the Lord was my strength and ^bmy song^b
when he became my salvation.

³ Then shall you rejoice in drawing water
from the fountains of salvation.

⁴ In that day you will say,
Give thanks to the Lord; invoke his name.

---

c15   Phrase transposed; in text follows *and smite it*

a2   Heb. *ʾel ʾēl;* so 1QIsaᵃ. A probable haplography in MT

b2   Heb. *zimrāt yā,* a probable dittography, emended to *zimrātî*

Make known his deeds among the nations;
    commemorate his exalted name.
⁵ Sing in praise of the Lord,
    who has performed wonders;
    let it be acknowledged throughout the earth!
⁶ Shout and sing for joy,
    O inhabitants of Zion,
for renowned among you
    is the Holy One of Israel.

13 An oracle concerning Babylon, which Isaiah the son of Amoz saw in vision:
    ² Raise the ensign on a barren mountain;
        sound the voice among them!
    Beckon them with the hand to advance
        into the precincts of the elite.
    ³ I have charged my holy ones,
        called out my valiant ones:
    ᶜmy anger is not uponᶜ those
        who take pride in me.

    ⁴ Hark! A tumult on the mountains,
        as of a vast multitude.
    Hark! An uproar among kingdoms,
        as of nations assembling:
    the Lord of Hosts is marshalling
        an army for war.
    ⁵ They come from a distant land
        beyond the horizon—
    the Lord and the instruments of his wrath—
        to cause destruction throughout the earth.

    ⁶ Lament, for the day of the Lord is near;
        it shall come as a violent blow
        from the Almighty.
    ⁷ Then shall every hand grow weak
        and the hearts of all men melt.

*c*3   Heb. *lᵉʾappî ʿallîzê*, exhibiting a double haplography, emended to *lōʾ ʾappî ʿal ʿallîzê*

⁸ They shall be terrified,
    in throes of agony,
  seized with trembling,
    like a woman in labor.
  Men will look at one another aghast,
    their faces set aflame.

⁹ The day of the Lord shall come
    as a cruel outburst of anger and wrath
  to make the earth a desolation,
    that sinners may be annihilated from it.
¹⁰ The stars and constellations of the heavens
    will not shine.
  When the sun rises, it shall be obscured,
    nor will the moon give its light.
¹¹ I have decreed calamity for the world,
    punishment for the wicked;
  I will put an end to the arrogance
    of insolent men
    and humble the pride of tyrants.
¹² I will make mankind scarcer than fine gold,
    men *more rare* than gold of Ophir.
¹³ I will cause disturbance in the heavens
    when the earth is jolted out of place
  by the anger of the Lord of Hosts,
    in the day of his blazing wrath.

¹⁴ Then, like a deer that is chased,
    or a flock of sheep that no one rounds up,
  each will return to his own people
    and everyone flee to his homeland.
¹⁵ Whoever is found shall be thrust through;
    all who are caught shall fall by the sword.
¹⁶ Their infants shall be dashed in pieces
    before their eyes,
  their homes plundered,
    their wives ravished.
¹⁷ See, I stir up against them the Medes,
    who do nor value silver nor covet gold.

¹⁸ Their bows shall tear apart the young.
>They will show no mercy to the newborn;
their eye will not look with compassion
>on children.
¹⁹ And Babylon, the most splendid of kingdoms,
>the glory and pride of Chaldeans,
shall be *thrown down*
>as God overthrew Sodom and Gomorrah.
²⁰ Never shall it be reinhabited;
>it shall not be resettled
>through all generations.
Nomads will not pitch their tents there,
>nor will shepherds rest their flocks in it.
²¹ But wild animals will infest it,
>and its buildings overflow with weasels;
birds of prey will find lodging there
>and demonic creatures prance about in it.
²² Jackals will cry out from its palaces,
>howling creatures from its amusement halls.
Her time draws near;
>*Babylon's*ᵈ days shall not be prolonged.

14 The Lord will have compassion on Jacob
>and once again choose Israel;
he will settle them in their own land,
>and proselytes will adhere to them
>and join the house of Jacob.
² The nations will take them
>and bring them to their own place.
And the house of Israel will possess them*ᵃ*
>as menservants and maidservants
>in the land of the Lord:
they will take captive their captors
>and rule over their oppressors.

---

d22   Heb. *Her*
a2   I.e., the nations

³In the day the Lord gives you relief from grief and anguish,
and from the arduous servitude imposed on you, ⁴you will
take up this taunt against the king of Babylon, and say,

> How the tyrant has met his end
> and tyranny*ᵇ* ceased!
> ⁵The Lord has broken the staff of the wicked,
> the rod of those who ruled—
> ⁶him who with unerring blows
> struck down the nations in anger,
> who subdued peoples in his wrath
> by relentless oppression.
> ⁷Now the whole earth is at rest and at peace;
> there is jubilant celebration!
> ⁸The pine trees, too, rejoice over you,
> as do the cedars of Lebanon:
> Since you have been laid low,
> no hewer has risen against us!

> ⁹Sheol below was in commotion because of you,
> anticipating your arrival;
> on your account it roused all the spirits
> of the world's leaders,
> causing all who had ruled nations
> to rise up from their thrones.
> ¹⁰All alike were moved to say to you,
> Even you have become powerless as we are!
> You have become like us!

> ¹¹Your glory has been cast down to Sheol,
> along with the music of your lyres.
> Beneath you is a bed of maggots;
> you are covered with worms.
> ¹²How you have fallen from the heavens,
> O morning star, son of the dawn!
> You who commanded the nations
> have been hewn down to earth!

---

*b*4   Or, *rage*; so 1QIsaᵃ; LXX. MT rendering is unknown.

¹³ You said in your heart,
    I will rise in the heavens
  and set up my throne
    above the stars of God;
  I will seat myself
    in the mount of assembly *of the gods*,
    in the utmost heights of Zaphon.
¹⁴ I will ascend
    above the altitude of the clouds;
    I will make myself like the Most High!
¹⁵ But you have been brought down to Sheol,
    to the utmost depths of the Pit.
¹⁶ Those who catch sight of you
    stare at you, wondering,
  Is this the man who made the earth shake
    and kingdoms quake,
¹⁷ who turned the world into a wilderness,
    demolishing its cities,
  permitting not his captives to return home?

¹⁸ All rulers of nations lie in state,
    each among his own kindred.
¹⁹ But you are cast away unburied
    like a repugnant fetus,
  exposed like the slain
    disfigured by the sword,
  whose mangled remains
    are thrown in a gravel pit.
²⁰ You shall not share burial with them,
    for you have destroyed your land
    and murdered your people.
  May the brood of miscreants
    never more be mentioned!
²¹ Prepare for the massacre of their sons,
    in consequence of their fathers' deeds,
  lest they rise up again
    and take possession of the world,
  and fill the face of the earth with cities.

²²I will rise up against them,
    says the Lord of Hosts.
I will cut off Babylon's name and remnant,
    its offspring and descendants, says the Lord.
²³I will turn it into swamplands,
    a haunt for ravens;
I will sweep it with the broom of destruction,
    says the Lord of Hosts.

²⁴The Lord of Hosts made an oath, saying,
    As I foresaw it, so shall it happen;
    as I planned it, so shall it be:
²⁵I will break Assyria in my own land,
    trample them underfoot on my mountains;
their yoke shall be taken from them,
    their burden removed from their shoulders.

²⁶These are things determined
    upon the whole earth;
this is the hand upraised
    over all nations.
²⁷For what the Lord of Hosts has determined,
    who shall revoke?
When his hand is upraised,
    who can turn it away?

²⁸In the year King Ahaz died, came this oracle:
    ²⁹Rejoice not, all you Philistines,
    now that the rod which struck you is broken.
From among the descendants of that snake
    shall spring up a viper,
and his offspring
    shall be a fiery flying serpent.
³⁰The elect poor shall have pasture,
    and the needy recline in safety.
But your descendants I will kill with famine,
    and your survivors shall be slain.

³¹ Wail at the gates; howl in the city!
    Utterly melt away, you Philistines!
  From the North shall come *pillars of* smoke,
    and no place he has designated shall evade it.
³² What shall then be told
    the envoys of the nation?
  The Lord has founded Zion;
    let his longsuffering people find refuge there.

15 An oracle concerning Moab:
    When in one night Ar is devastated,
      Moab shall be silenced;
    when in one night Kir is razed,
      Moab shall be destroyed.
² They will go up to the sanctuaries,
    and in Dibon to the hill shrines, to weep;
    they will wail in Moab over Nebo and Medeba.
  Every head shall be bald,
    every beard cut off.
³ They will wear sackcloth openly;
    on the housetops and in the streets
  they will altogether wail
    and give way to weeping.
⁴ Heshbon will cry for help, as will Elealeh;
    their appeal shall be heard as far as Jahaz.
  They will sound the alarm
    to summon the armed men of Moab,
  but their spirit shall be broken.

⁵ My heart will cry out for Moab;
    its fugitives will reach Zoar
    and as far as Eglath Shelishiah.
  In tears they will ascend
    the slopes of Luhith;
  on the road to Horonaim
    they will raise the cry of catastrophe.
⁶ For the waters of Nimrim shall be desolate;
    the grass shall dry up,

vegetation disappear,
and no green foliage shall remain.
⁷ The surplus they have acquired,
and their personal belongings,
they will carry away
over the Valley of the Willows.
⁸ The cry of calamity
shall encompass the land of Moab;
the sound of it shall reach Eglaim
and echo as far as Beer Elim.
⁹ Although the waters of Dibon
shall flow with blood,
yet will I impose more than this
upon Dibon:
I will bring lions upon the fugitives of Moab
and on those who remain in the land.

16 Send couriers to those who rule in the earth,
from Sela in the desert
to the mountain of the Daughter of Zion.
² Like fluttering birds forced out of the nest,
so are Moab's women at the fords of Arnon.
³ Provide a solution, *they say*;
judge our case!
Overshadow us at high noon
as though it were night!
Shelter those dispossessed;
betray not the refugees!
⁴ Let the exiles of Moab dwell with you;
be a refuge to them from the aggressors!

When oppressors are no more
and violence has ceased,
when tyrants are destroyed from the earth,
⁵ then, in loving kindness,
shall a throne be set up
in the abode of David,
and in faithfulness a judge sit on it

who will maintain justice
and expedite righteousness.

⁶ We have heard of the glories of Moab,
of its excessive pride and its boasting,
and of its outbursts of false propaganda.
⁷ For this shall the Moabites *be made to* lament,
and all *have cause to* bewail Moab:
they shall groan at the ruin of Kir Hareseth
in utter dejection.

⁸ For the vineyards of Heshbon shall wither;
the ruling nations will smite Sibma's vines.
Its runner vines reached Jazer,
trailing through the desert;
its branches spread abroad across the sea.
⁹ Therefore I will mourn as Jazer mourns
for the vines of Sibmah;
I will water you with my tears,
O Heshbon and Elealeh,
when your shouts of cheer
over the summer fruit and harvest
are stilled.
¹⁰ The joyful festivity will be gone
from the orchards;
no shouts of delight shall sound
in the vineyards.
The wine treaders will tread no wine
in the presses;
the vintage shout
I will bring to an end.

¹¹ My breast will vibrate like a harp for Moab,
my inmost being for Kir Hareseth.
¹² For when the Moabites weary themselves
with petitioning on the hill shrines,
and enter their sanctuaries to pray,
it shall be to no avail.

¹³ These things the Lord spoke hitherto about Moab. ¹⁴ But now the Lord has said, Within three years, as the term of a lease, Moab's glory shall become ignominy. For all its large populace there shall be very few left, and those of no account.

17 An oracle concerning Damascus:
   Damascus shall cease to be a city
   and become a heap of ruins.
  ² The cities of Aroer shall lie forsaken
   and become places for herds to recline,
  where no one will disturb them.
  ³ When Ephraim's defense comes to an end,
   so shall the sovereignty of Damascus:
  as with the glory of the children of Israel,
   so shall it be with Aram's remnant,
  says the Lord of Hosts.

  ⁴ In that day Jacob's glory shall wane,
   and his fatness of body become leanness.
  ⁵ After being like a harvest of ripe grain,
   whose ears are reaped by the armful,
  he will become like ears plucked
   in the Valley of Rephaim,
   ⁶ when only the gleanings are left,
  or when an olive tree is beaten,
   having two or three berries
   in the topmost bough,
  or four or five in its most fruitful branch,
   says the Lord, the God of Israel.

  ⁷ In that day men will have regard
   to their Maker,
  and their eyes look
   to the Holy One of Israel,
  ⁸ and regard not the altars,
   the works of their hands,
  nor look to things made by their fingers—
   the idols of prosperity and the shining images.

⁹ In that day their mighty cities shall be like the deserted
towns of the *ᵃHivites and Amorites,ᵃ* which they abandoned
before the Israelites during the desolation.

¹⁰ For you have forgotten your God,
    your salvation,
and not remembered the Rock,
    your fortress.
Therefore, though you plant choice crops
    and sow hybrid seed,
¹¹ and though you make them thrive
    the day you plant them,
causing them to sprout
    the very morning you sow them,
yet the harvest shall vanish
    in a day of diseases and incurable pain.

¹² Woe to the many peoples in an uproar,
    who rage like the raging of the seas—
tumultuous nations, in commotion
    like the turbulence of mighty waters!
¹³ Nations may roar
    like the roaring of great waters,
but when he rebukes them
    they will flee far away;
they will be driven before the wind
    like chaff on the mountains,
    or as whirling *dust* in a storm.
¹⁴ At evening time shall be the catastrophe,
    and before morning they shall be no more.
This is the lot of those who plunder us,
    the fate of those who despoil us.

18   Woe to the land of buzzing wings
        beyond the rivers of Cush,
    ² which sends emissaries by sea,
        in swift craft across the water.

---

*a*9   So LXX; MT reads *groves and treetops*

> *They say*, Go speedily, you messengers!
>> *Go* to a people perpetually on the move,
> a nation dreaded far and wide,
>> a people continually infringing,
>> whose rivers have annexed their lands.

³ All you who live in the world,
>> you inhabitants of the earth,
> look to the ensign
>> when it is lifted up in the mountains;
>> heed the trumpet when sounded!
⁴ For thus said the Lord to me:
> I will watch in silence
> over my dwelling place
> when the searing heat
>> overtakes the reapers,ᵃ
> and when the rainclouds *appear*
> amid the fever of reaping.
⁵ For before the harvest,
>> when the *time of* flowering is past
> and the set blossoms are developing
>> into young fruit,
> they will cut down the fruit-bearing twigs
>> with knives
> and remove the new branches
>> by slashing.
⁶ All shall be left to the birds of prey
> of the mountains,
>> and to the beasts of the land;
> the birds of prey will feed on them all summer
>> and the beasts of the land all winter.

⁷ At that time shall tribute be brought
> to the Lord of Hosts
> from a nation perpetually on the move,
>> from a nation dreaded far and wide,

---

*a*4   Heb. *ʾôr, light,* emended to *ʾôreh*

a people continually infringing,
    whose rivers have annexed their lands,
to the place of the name of the Lord of Hosts:
    Mount Zion.

19 An oracle concerning Egypt:
    When the Lord enters Egypt
        riding on swift clouds,
    the idols of Egypt will rock at his presence,
        and the Egyptians' hearts melt within them.
²I will stir up the Egyptians
    against the Egyptians;
they will fight brother against brother
    and neighbor against neighbor,
city against city
    and state against state.
³Egypt's spirit shall be drained from within;
    I will frustrate their plans,
and they will resort to the idols
    and to spiritists,
    to mediums and witchcraft.
⁴Then will I deliver the Egyptians
    into the hand of a cruel master;
a harsh ruler will subject them,
    says my Lord, the Lord of Hosts.

⁵The waters of the lakes shall ebb away
    as stream beds become desolate and dry.
⁶The rivers shall turn foul,
    and Egypt's waterways recede and dry up.
Reeds and rushes shall wither;
    ⁷vegetation adjoining canals and estuaries,
and all things sown along irrigation channels,
    shall shrivel and blow away and be no more.
⁸Fishermen will deplore *their lot*
    and anglers in canals bemoan themselves;
those who cast nets on water
    will be in misery.

⁹Manufacturers of combed linen
and weavers of fine fabrics
will be dismayed.
¹⁰The textile workers will know despair,
and all who work for wages ªsuffer distress.ª

¹¹The ministers of Zoan are utter fools;
the wisest of Pharoah's advisers
give absurd counsel.
How can you say to Pharoah,
We ourselves are as wise as the first rulers?
¹²Where are your wise men indeed?
Let them please tell you,
if they can discern it,
what the Lord of Hosts has in mind
for Egypt!
¹³The ministers of Zoan have been foolish,
the officials of Noph deluded;
the heads of state have led Egypt astray.
¹⁴The Lord has permeated them
with a spirit of confusion;
they have misled Egypt in all that it does,
causing it to stagger like a drunkard
into his vomit.
¹⁵And there shall be nothing the Egyptians
can do about it,
neither head nor tail, palm top or reed.

¹⁶In that day the Egyptians will be as women, fearful and
afraid at the brandishing hand the Lord of Hosts wields over
them. ¹⁷The land of Judah shall become a source of terror
to the Egyptians; all reminded of it shall dread what the
Lord of Hosts has in store for them.
¹⁸In that day five Hebrew-speaking cities in the land of
Egypt will swear loyalty to the Lord of Hosts. One shall be
known as the City of Righteousness.ᵇ

a10   Heb. ᵓagmê nepeš, ponds for life, emended to ᶜagmê nepeš
b18   So LXX; MT reads city of destruction, 1QIsaª city of the sun

¹⁹ In that day there shall be an altar *erected* to the Lord in the midst of the land of Egypt and a monument to the Lord at its border. ²⁰ They shall serve as a sign and testimony of the Lord of Hosts in the land of Egypt: when they cry out to the Lord because of the oppressors, he will send them a savior, who will take up their cause and deliver them.

²¹ The Lord will make himself known to the Egyptians, and the Egyptians shall know the Lord in that day. They will worship by sacrifice and offerings, and make vows to the Lord and fulfill them. ²² The Lord will smite Egypt, and by smiting heal it: they will turn back to the Lord, and he will respond to their pleas and heal them.

²³ In that day there shall be a highway from Egypt to Assyria. Assyrians shall come to Egypt and Egyptians go to Assyria, and the Egyptians shall labor with the Assyrians.

²⁴ In that day Israel shall be the third party to Egypt and to Assyria, a blessing in the midst of the earth. ²⁵ The Lord of Hosts will bless them, saying, Blessed by Egypt my people, Assyria the work of my hands, and Israel my inheritance.

20 In the year the general who was sent by Sargon king of Assyria came to Ashdod and took it by combat, ² the Lord had spoken through Isaiah the son of Amoz, saying, Go and ungird the sackcloth from your loins and remove the shoes from your feet. And he had done so, going naked and barefoot.

³ Then the Lord said, Just as my servant Isaiah has gone naked and barefoot for three years as a sign and portent against Egypt and Cush, ⁴ so shall the king of Assyria lead away the captives of Egypt and the exiles of Cush, both young and old, naked and barefoot, with buttocks uncovered—to Egypt's shame. ⁵ Men shall be appalled and perplexed at Cush, their hope, and at Egypt, their boast.

⁶ In that day shall the inhabitants of this isle say, See what has become of those we looked up to, on whom we relied[a] for help and deliverance from the king of Assyria! How shall we ourselves escape?

*a*6   So 1QIsaᵃ; MT reads *to whom we fled*

21 An oracle concerning the Wilderness of the West:
Like tornadoes sweeping through the South,
they come from the steppes,
a land of terror.

² A grim vision has been revealed to me:
the traitor in the act of treachery,
the destroyer laying waste.
Attack, O Elamites! Lay siege, you Medes!
All the sighing that *Babylon*ᵃ has caused
I will bring to an end.

³ Therefore my whole frame is racked
with trembling;
throes of agony have seized me
like a woman in labor.
I am tormented beyond giving heed;
I am too distraught to see.
⁴ My mind reels, I am paralyzed with fear;
the nightfall I longed for
has become a horror to me:
⁵ They prepare tables;
they deck them with candlesticks.
They are eating and drinking...
Mobilize, you commanders! Oil the armor!

⁶ Because of this my Lord said to me,
Go and appoint a watchman
who will report what he sees.
⁷ Let him watch for chariots with teams of horses,
riders on asses and riders on camels.
He must be most vigilant, fully alert.

⁸ Then the lookoutᵇ cried,
I have been standing on the watchtower
day in and day out, my Lord;
night after night I have stood guard.

*a*2   Heb. *she*
*b*8   So 1QIsaᵃ; MT reads *a lion*

⁹ Now they come:
>cavalry and teams of horses!
And he gave the reply,
>She has fallen; Babylon has fallen.
All her idol gods
>he has razed to the ground.

¹⁰ ^cTo you who know me, who are of my fold,^c
>I have reported what I heard
from the Lord of Hosts, the God of Israel.

¹¹ An oracle concerning Dumah:
>Men call to me from Seir,
>>Watchman, what remains of the night?
>>Watchman, how much of the night is left?
¹² The watchman replies,
>>Morning comes, though it is still night.
>If you would ascertain it,
>>do so by repenting and coming back.

¹³ An oracle concerning those in Arabia:
>You wandering bands of Dedanites,
>>who sojourn in the forests of Arabia,
¹⁴ bring water to greet the thirsty;
>>meet the fugitives with food,
>>O inhabitants of the land of Tema.
¹⁵ For they flee from destruction,
>>from the bared sword, the drawn bow
>>and the severity of war.

¹⁶ On account of this, my Lord said to me, Within a year, as the term of a lease, Kedar's glory shall fully expire. ¹⁷ And the number of valiant archers remaining of the sons of Kedar shall be few. The Lord, the God of Israel, has spoken it.

*c*10   So 1QIsa^a; MT reads *My threshed and winnowed ones*

22 An oracle concerning the Arena of Spectacles:
Whatever is the matter with you,
    causing you all at once
    to climb onto the housetops?
² You resounded with loud cheers—
    a tumultuous town, a city of revelry!
But your slain were not killed by the sword;
    they did not die in battle!
³ Your chiefs, altogether in flight,
    are captured without using the bow;
all those of you left behind are caught easily
    before you can get away.
⁴ Because of this I said,
    Turn your attention from me,
    though I weep bitterly;
hasten not to comfort me
    at the ruin of the Daughter of my People.

⁵ For my Lord, the Lord of Hosts, has in store
    a day of commotion and trampling and riot
in the Arena of Spectacles,
    a day of battering down walls,
and of crying in distress,
    To the mountains!
⁶ When Elam takes up the quiver,
    and horses are harnessed
to the chariots of Aram,*a*
    and Kir uncovers the armor,
⁷ then shall your choice valleys
    fill with chariots,
and cavalry take up positions
    at your gateways.
⁸ And in the day Judea's defensive screen
    is removed,
you will look to the forest home
    as protection.

*a*6   Heb. *ʾādām, man/men,* emended to *ʾārām*

⁹ When you saw the city of David
    increasingly breached,
  you conserved water
    in the Lower Reservoir.
¹⁰ You took a census of the buildings in Jerusalem,
    tearing down buildings to fortify your wall.
¹¹ You built cisterns between the walls
    for the water from the Old Reservoir,
  but you did not look to its Maker,
    nor have regard for the One who designed it
    long ago.
¹² In such a day my Lord,
    the Lord of Hosts,
  calls for weeping and lamentation,
    for austerity and wearing sackcloth.
¹³ Instead, there is mirth and merrymaking,
    the killing of cattle and slaughter of sheep,
  eating meat and drinking wine:
    Let us dine and drink, for tomorrow we die!
¹⁴ The Lord of Hosts revealed this to my ears: Such wickedness cannot be forgiven you till you die, says my Lord, the Lord of Hosts.

¹⁵ Thus said my Lord, the Lord of Hosts:
    Go and see that steward, Shebna,
    overseer of the palace.
¹⁶ *Say to him,* What are you up to?
    Who do you think you are,
  that you have hewn yourself a tomb here,
    like those who hew their sepulchres up high,
  carving out graves for themselves
    in the rock?
¹⁷ The Lord will hurl you away
    as an athlete hurls a missile;
    he will make you soar like a dart.
¹⁸ He will bind you tightly about
    and send you spinning like a top
    into an open country.

> There shall you die,
> > and your glorious conveyance there
> > shall be a disgrace to your master's house.
> ¹⁹ I will thrust you out of office;
> > you will be expelled from your post.

²⁰ In that day I will commission my servant Eliakim the son of Hilkiah: ²¹I will clothe him with your robe and bind your girdle on him; I will appoint him your jurisdiction. And he will be a father to the inhabitants of Jerusalem and to the house of Judah.²² I will invest him with the keys of the house of David: when he opens none shall shut, when he shuts none shall open. ²³I will fasten him as a nail in a sure place, and he will be a throne of glory to the house of his father. ²⁴Upon him shall be hung all the glory of his father's house: his descendants and posterity, including all the lesser vessels, from ordinary bowls to the most common containers.

²⁵ In that day, says the Lord of Hosts, the nail that was fastened in a sure place shall be removed. It shall be dislodged and fall, and the burden hanging on it cut off. The Lord has spoken it.

23 An oracle concerning Tyre:
> > Sound your sirens, O merchant ships!
> > > For *Tyre*^a is laid waste,
> > > stripped of warehouse and wharf.
> > > *On their way* from the land of Kittim
> > > they shall be informed of it.
> > ² Be dumbfounded, you inhabitants of the isles,
> > > who were amply replenished
> > > by the traders of Sidon crossing the seas.
> > ³ The grain of Shihor,
> > > the harvest of the Nile,
> > > was her source of revenue upon the high seas
> > > when she became the merchant of nations.

*a*1   Heb. *she*

60

⁴Be dismayed, O Sidon, because the Sea,
 the mighty haven of the Sea, has declared,
I no longer labor and bear children!
 I no longer rear young men or raise virgins!
⁵When the news of Tyre reaches Egypt,
 men will be in anguish at the report.

⁶Move on to Tarshish lamenting,
 you inhabitants of the isles.
⁷Is this your festive *city* of ancient origin,
 whose feet led her to settle far-off *lands?*
⁸Who devised this strategem against Tyre,
 the imperial *city,*
whose traders were princes,
 whose merchants the world's celebrities?
⁹The Lord of Hosts devised it,
 to make all glorying in excellence a profanity,
and the world's celebrities an utter execration.

¹⁰Overflow your land like the Nile,
 O Daughter of Tarshish:
 the harbor is no more.
¹¹The Lord will stretch out his hand over the Sea
 and distress kingdoms;
he will give orders concerning the merchant *city*
 that her ports of haven be destroyed.
¹²He will say, You will frolic no more,
 O ravished virgin, Daughter of Sidon.
Get up and cross over to Kittim,
 though even there you will find no rest.
¹³So too with the land of the Chaldeans,
 the people who founded *Tyre*[b] for shipping.
Was it not the Assyrians
 who set up observatories,
exposed its fortifications,
 and caused its downfall?

*b*13 Heb. *her*

> ¹⁴ Sound your sirens, O merchant ships;
> your haven is desolate!

¹⁵ In that day Tyre shall be forgotten seventy years, the lifetime of a king. And at the end of seventy years, Tyre shall be as the harlot in the song:

> ¹⁶ Take a lyre and go about the town,
> O forgotten harlot.
> Play skillfully; sing song after song,
> that you may be remembered.

¹⁷ For after seventy years, the Lord will revisit Tyre. And she will return to her trade, and hire herself out to all the kingdoms of the world on the face of the earth. ¹⁸ Her merchandise and hire shall be consecrated to the Lord; it shall not be hoarded or stored up. Her commerce shall provide for those who dwell in the presence of the Lord, that they may eat their fill and be elegantly clothed.

24

> Lo! The Lord will lay waste the earth
> and empty it;
> he will disfigure its surface
> and scatter its inhabitants.
> ² And it shall be with priest as with people,
> with master as with servant,
> with mistress as with maid,
> with seller as with buyer,
> with borrower as with lender,
> with debtor as with creditor—
> ³ when the earth is sacked,
> it shall be utterly ravaged.
> The Lord has given word concerning it.

> ⁴ The earth shall pine away,
> the world miserably perish;
> the elite of the earth shall be made wretched.
> ⁵ The earth lies polluted under its inhabitants:
> they have transgressed the laws,

changed the ordinances,
    set at nought the ancient covenant.
⁶ The curse devours the earth,
    for those who dwell on it have incurred guilt;
because of it the population of the earth
    shall be diminished*a*
    and little of mankind remain.

⁷ The new wine withers on languishing vines,
    making all the lighthearted lament.
⁸ The rhythm of drums ceases,
    the revelers' din stops;
    the pulsating of lyres comes to an end.
⁹ Men no longer drink wine amid song;
    liquor has turned bitter to drinkers.
¹⁰ The towns of disorder are broken up;
    all houses are shuttered,
    that none may enter.
¹¹ Outside is *heard* the clamor for wine,
    but all joy has become gloom:
    the earth's vitality is gone.
¹² Havoc remains in the city;
    the gates lie battered to ruin.

¹³ Then shall it happen in the earth
    among the nations
as when an olive tree is beaten,
    or as grapes are gleaned
    when the vintage is ended.
¹⁴ Then will these lift up their voice
    and shout for joy,
and *those* from across the sea
    exult at the Lord's ingenuity.
¹⁵ Because of it they will give glory to the Lord
    in the regions of sunrise,
and in the isles of the sea
    to the name of the Lord, the God of Israel.

*a*6   So 1QIsaᵃ; MT reads *burned*

¹⁶ From a sector of the earth we hear singing:
    Glorious are the righteous!
  Whereas I thought, I am wasting away;
    I am weakening:
  woe is me; the traitors have been treacherous,
    the turncoats have deceitfully betrayed!

¹⁷ Terrors and pitfalls and traps await you,
    O inhabitants of the earth:
¹⁸ those who flee at the sound of terror
    shall fall into a pit,
  and those who get up from the pit
    shall be caught in a trap.
  For when the windows on high are opened,
    the earth shall shake to its foundations.

¹⁹ The earth shall be crushed and rent;
    the earth shall break up and cave in;
    the earth shall convulse and lurch.
²⁰ The earth shall reel to and fro like a drunkard,
    sway back and forth like a shanty;
  its transgressions weigh it down,
    and when it falls it shall rise no more.

²¹ In that day will the Lord deal on high
    with the hosts on high
    and on earth with the rulers of the earth.
²² They shall be herded together
    like prisoners to a dungeon
  and shut in confinement many days,
    as punishment.
²³ The moon will blush
    and the sun be put to shame,
  when the Lord of Hosts manifests his reign
    in Mount Zion and in Jerusalem,
  and *his* glory in the presence of his elders.

25

In that day you will say,
    O Lord, thou art my God;
I will extol thee by praising thy name.
    For with perfect faithfulness
thou hast performed wonders,
    things planned of old.
² Thou hast made the city a heap of rubble,
    fortified towns a ruin—
heathen mansions shall no more form cities,
    nor ever be rebuilt!
³ For this will powerful peoples revere thee,
    a community of tyrannous nations fear thee.
⁴ Thou wast a refuge for the poor,
    a shelter for the needy in distress,
a covert from the downpour
    and shade from the heat.
When the blasts of tyrants beat down
    like torrents against a wall,
⁵ or like scorching heat in the desert,
    thou didst quell the onslaughts
    of the heathen:
as burning heat by the shade of a cloud,
    thou subduest the power of tyrants.

⁶ In this mountain will the Lord of Hosts prepare
    a sumptuous feast for all peoples,
a feast of leavened cakes,
    succulent and delectable,
    of matured wines well refined.
⁷ In this mountain he will destroy
    the veil that veils all peoples,
the shroud that shrouds all nations,
    ⁸ by abolishing Death forever.
My Lord the Lord will wipe away
    the tears from all faces;
he will remove the reproach of his people
    from throughout the earth.
The Lord has spoken it.

⁹ In that day you*a* will say,
This is our God,
whom we expected would save us.
This is the Lord for whom we have waited;
let us joyfully celebrate his salvation!

¹⁰ For in this mountain rests the hand of the Lord,
and under him Moab shall be trampled down
as straw is trampled in a dung pit.
¹¹ For when he stretches his hands
into the midst of it,
as a swimmer spreads his hands to swim,
he will pull down his pride in the attempt.
¹² Your highly walled fortifications
he will lay low by razing them to the ground,
even with the dust.

26 In that day shall this song be sung in the land of Judah:
Our city is strong; salvation he has set up
as walls and barricades!
² Open the gates to let in the nation
righteous because it keeps faith.
³ Those whose minds are steadfast, *O Lord*,
thou preservest in perfect peace,
for in thee they are secure.
⁴ Ever trust in the Lord,
for the Lord Yah is an everlasting Rock.
⁵ He has put down the elite inhabitants
of the exalted city
by casting it to the ground,
laying it even with the dust.
⁶ It is trodden underfoot
by the feet of the poor,
by the footsteps of those impoverished.

*a*9   So 1QIsaᵃ; MT reads *he*

⁷The path of the righteous is straight;
    thou pavest an undeviating course
    for the upright.
⁸In the very passage of thine ordinances
    we anticipate thee, O Lord;
    the soul's desire is to contemplate thy name.
⁹My soul yearns for thee in the night;
    at daybreak my spirit within me
    seeks after thee.
For when thine ordinances are on the earth,
    the inhabitants of the world
    learn righteousness.
¹⁰Though favor be shown the wicked,
    they will not learn righteousness;
in a land of uprightness they remain perverse
    and see not the glory of the Lord.
¹¹O Lord, thy hand is lifted up,
    but they perceive it not.
Let them perceive with dismay
    thy zeal for thy people,
when the fire prepared for thine enemies
    consumes them.

¹²O Lord, thou bringest about our peace;
    even all that we have accomplished
    thou hast done for us.
¹³O Lord, our God, lords other than thou
    have ruled over us,
    but thee alone we recall by name.
¹⁴They are dead, to live no more,
    spirits who will not rise up;
thou appointest them to destruction,
    wiping out all recollection of them.
¹⁵Thou hast enlarged the nation, O Lord,
    and by enlarging it gained glory for thyself;
thou hast withdrawn all borders in the earth.

¹⁶ O Lord, in their distress they remembered thee;
    they poured out silent prayers
    when thy chastisements were upon them.
¹⁷ As a woman about to give birth
    cries out from her pangs during labor,
    so were we at thy presence, O Lord.
¹⁸ We were with child; we have been in labor,
    but have brought forth only wind.
We have not wrought salvation in the earth,
    that the inhabitants of the world
    might not fall.

¹⁹ Yet shall thy dead live
    when their bodies*a* arise.
Thou wilt say to them,
    Awake, and sing for joy,
you who abide in the dust:
    your dew is the dew of sunrise!
    For the earth shall cast up its dead.
²⁰ Come, O my people, enter your chambers
    and shut the doors behind you;
hide yourselves a little while
    until the wrath is past.
²¹ For now will the Lord
    come out of his dwelling place
to punish the inhabitants of the earth
    for their iniquities;
the earth will uncover the blood shed upon it
    and no more conceal its slain.

27

In that day will the Lord,
    with his great and powerful sword,
punish severely*a* Leviathan,
    the evasive maritime serpent,
Leviathan, that devious sea monster,
    when he slays the dragons of the Sea.

*a*19   Heb. *my body*. MT evidences incomplete third person pronoun suffix; cf. LXX
*a*1   Term modifies *sword* in the text, an incongruity in translation

² In that day, sing of *the earth*^b
  as of a delightful vineyard
  ³ of which I, the Lord, am keeper.
I water it constantly,
  watch over it night and day,
  lest anything be amiss.
⁴ I have no more anger *toward her*.
  Should briars and thorns come up,
 I will ruthlessly attack them
  and altogether set them ablaze.
⁵ But should they take hold of me for a refuge
  and make peace with me,
  they shall be reconciled to me.
⁶ For *in days* to come, when Jacob takes root
  and Israel bursts into blossom,
 the face of the earth shall fill with fruit.

⁷ Was he smitten as were his smiters?
  Or was he slain as were they who slew him?
⁸ Thou hast dealt with them
  by utterly banishing them, *O Lord*.
By his fierce blast they were flung away
  in the day of the burning east wind.
⁹ But by this shall Jacob's iniquity be expiated,
  as a result of this his sins removed:
when he makes like crushed chalkstone
  all altar stones,
leaving no idols of prosperity
  and shining images standing.
¹⁰ Because *of them* the fortified cities lie forlorn,
  deserted habitations,
  forsaken like a wilderness;
steers forage and recline there,
  stripping bare the young branches *of trees*.
¹¹ A harvest of twigs dries, broken off by women
  who come to light their fires with them.

b2 Heb. *her*; cf. 26.21; 27.6

> They are not a discerning people;
>> therefore their Maker shows them no mercy:
>> he who formed them favors them not.

¹² In that day the Lord will thresh out *his harvest* from the torrent of the River to the streams of Egypt. But you shall be gleaned one by one, O children of Israel.
¹³ In that day a loud trumpet shall sound, and they who were lost in the land of Assyria and they who were out-casts in the land of Egypt shall come and bow down to the Lord in the holy mountain at Jerusalem.

28

> Woe to the garlands of glory
>> of the drunkards of Ephraim!
> Their crowning splendor has become
>> as fading wreaths
> on the heads of *a*the opulent*a*
>> overcome with wine.
> ² My Lord has in store one mighty and strong:
>> as a ravaging hailstorm sweeping down,
> or like an inundating deluge of mighty waters,
>> he will hurl them to the ground by his hand.
> ³ The proud garlands of the drunkards of Ephraim
>> shall be trodden underfoot.
> ⁴ And the fading wreaths, the crowns of glory
>> on the heads of *a*the opulent,*a*
> shall be like the first-ripe fruit
>> before summer *harvest*:
> he who sees it
>> devours it the moment he has hold of it.

> ⁵ In that day shall the Lord of Hosts
>> be as a crown of beauty
> and wreath of glory
>> to the remnant of his people:
> ⁶ a spirit of justice
>> to him who sits in judgment,

*a*1, *a*4   Heb. *gêʾê šĕmānîm;* so 1QIsaᵃ. MT reads *gêʾ šĕmānîm. fat gully/ravine*

a source of strength
    to those who repulse the attack at the gates.

⁷ These too have indulged in wine
    and are giddy with strong drink:
priests and prophets have gone astray
    through liquor.
They are intoxicated with wine
    and stagger because of strong drink;
they err as seers,
    they blunder in their decisions.
⁸ For all tables are filled with vomit;
    no spot is without excrement.

⁹ Whom shall *the Lord*ᵇ give instruction?
    Whom shall he enlighten with revelation?
Weanlings weaned from milk,
    those just taken from the breast?
¹⁰ For it is *still* precept upon precept,
    precept upon precept,
measure by measure, measure by measure;
    a trifle here, a trifle there.

¹¹ Therefore, by incomprehensible speech
    and a strange tongue
    must he speak to these people,
¹² to whom he said,
    This is rest; let the weary rest!
This is a respite!
    But they would not listen.
¹³ So to them the word of the Lord remained:
    Precept upon precept, precept upon precept,
measure by measure, measure by measure;
    a trifle here, a trifle there, that,
persisting, they might lapse into stumbling
    and break themselves,
become ensnared and be taken captive.

*b*9   Heb. *he*

¹⁴ Therefore hear the word of the Lord,
>   you scoffers who preside over these people
>   in Jerusalem.
¹⁵ You have supposed,
>   by taking refuge in deception
>   and hiding behind falsehoods,
> to have covenanted with Death,
>   or reached an understanding with Sheol,
> that, should a flooding scourge
>   sweep through *the earth*,
> it shall not reach you.

¹⁶ Therefore, thus says my Lord the Lord:
>   I lay in Zion a stone, a keystone,
> a precious cornerstone, a sure foundation.
>   They who believe it will not do rashly.
¹⁷ I will make justice the measure,
>   righteousness the weight;
> a hail shall sweep away your false refuge
>   and waters flood the hiding place.
¹⁸ Your covenant with Death shall prove void,[c]
>   your understanding with Sheol have no effect:
> when the flooding scourge sweeps through,
>   you shall be overrun by it.
¹⁹ As often as it sweeps through,
>   you shall be seized by it:
> morning after morning it shall sweep through,
>   by day and by night *it shall seize you*;
> it shall cause terror merely to hear word of it.

²⁰ *Then shall come to pass the proverb:*
>   The couch is too short to stretch out on,
>   the covering too narrow to wrap oneself in.
²¹ For the Lord will rise up
>   as he did on Mount Perazim,
> and be stirred to anger,
>   as in the Valley of Gibeon—

c18   Heb. *kuppar, expiated,* emended to *ḥūpar*

to perform his act, his unwonted act,
and do his work, his bizarre work.
²² Now therefore scoff not,
lest your bonds grow severe,
for I have heard utter destruction
decreed by my Lord, the Lord of Hosts,
upon the whole earth.
²³ Give heed, and hear my voice!
Be attentive, and listen to what I say!
²⁴ Will the plowman be forever plowing
to sow seed,
disking and harrowing the same ground?
²⁵ When he has smoothed its surface,
does he not sprinkle fennel
and scatter cumin?
Does he not demarcate wheat from barley
and *plant* buckwheat in its own plot?
²⁶ His God instructs him,
directing him in the proper procedure.

²⁷ Fennel is not threshed
with a sharp-toothed sledge,
nor is a cartwheel rolled over cumin:
fennel is beaten out with a stick
and cumin with a rod.
²⁸ Domestic grain is ground;
one does not go on endlessly threshing it.
It cannot be ground
by driving horse and threshing cart *over it.*
²⁹ These things originate with the Lord of Hosts,
whose counsel is wonderful,
whose inspiration is surpassing.

29 Woe to Ariel—
Ariel, the city where David lodged!
Though you add year to year,
and the feastdays recur in succession,

73

²yet will I distress Ariel:
>there shall be mourning and sorrow
>>when she becomes as *my altar hearth.*

³I will encamp against you round about,
>and beleaguer you with assault posts,
>and erect siege installations against you.

⁴And when you have been laid low,
>you will speak from the ground,
>your words uttering out of the dust:
>your voice from the ground
>>shall be like that of a medium;
>>your sayings shall whisper out of the dust.

⁵Suddenly, in an instant,
>your crowds of evildoers*b*
>shall become as fine dust,
>>your violent mobs like flying chaff.

⁶She shall be chastened by the Lord of Hosts
>with thunderous quakings,
>resounding booms, tempestuous blasts
>>and conflagrations of devouring flame.

⁷And the nations amassed to fight against Ariel,
>all who congregate at her stronghold
>to distress her,
>>shall be as a dream seen in the night:

⁸like a hungry man who dreams he eats,
>but awakens famished,
>or like a thirsty man who dreams he drinks,
>but wakes up faint and craving.
>So shall be all the nations
>>that amass to fight against Mount Zion.

⁹Procrastinate, and become bewildered;
>preoccupy yourselves, until you cry for help.
>Be drunk, but not with wine;
>>stagger, but not from strong drink.

---

*a*2   Or, *Ariel,* a wordplay
*b*5   So 1QIsaᵃ; LXX. MT reads *of strangers*

¹⁰ The Lord has poured out on you
  a spirit of deep sleep:
he has shut your eyes, the prophets;
  he has covered your heads, the seers.

¹¹ For you the sum of vision has become as the words of a
sealed book which they give to one who is learned, saying,
Please read this, and he answers, I cannot; it is sealed.
¹² Or if they give it to one who is unlearned, saying,
Please read this, he answers, I am unlearned.

¹³ But my Lord says, Because these people
  approach me with the mouth
and pay me homage with their lips,
  while their heart remains far from me—
their piety toward me consisting of
  commandments of men learned by rote—
¹⁴ therefore it is
  that I continue to astound these people
  with wonder upon wonder,
rendering void the knowledge of their sages,
  the intelligence of their wise men insignificant.

¹⁵ Woe to those who contrive
  to hide their schemes from the Lord!
They work in the dark, thinking,
  Who will see us? Who will know?
¹⁶ What a contradiction you are!
  Shall the potter be regarded as the clay?
Shall what is made say of its maker,
  He did not make me,
or a work of its designer,
  He doesn't understand?
¹⁷ In a very little while, shall not Lebanon
  again become a fruitful land,
and lands now fruitful be considered backwoods?

¹⁸ In that day shall the deaf hear
  the words of the book

and the eyes of the blind see
out of gross darkness.
¹⁹ The lowly shall obtain an increase of joy
in the Lord,
and the poorest men rejoice
in the Holy One of Israel.
²⁰ For tyrants shall come to nought
and scorners cease;
all who persist in wickedness
shall be cut off—
²¹ those who at a word adjudge a man to be guilty,
who ensnare the defender at court,
who for nothing turn away
him who is in the right.

²² Therefore thus says the Lord,
who redeemed Abraham,
to the house of Jacob:
No longer shall Jacob be dismayed;
his face shall pale no more.
²³ For when he sees among him his children,
the work of my hands,
hallowing my name,
devoted to the Holy One of Jacob,
reverencing the God of Israel,
²⁴ then will the erring in spirit
gain understanding
and they who murmured
accept instruction.

30 Woe to you, rebellious sons, says the Lord,
for drawing up plans, but not by me,
for making alliances without my approval,
only adding sin to sin!
² They are bent on going down to Egypt—
but have not inquired at my mouth—
on seeking protection in Pharoah's forces,
on taking shelter in Egypt's shadow.

³ But Pharoah's protection
    shall turn to your shame,
  shelter in Egypt's shadow
    to embarrassment.
⁴ For all their officials at Zoan,
    and their envoys' travels to Hanes,
⁵ they shall be utterly disgusted
    with a people who will avail them nothing;
  they shall be of no help or benefit,
    but a humiliation and disgrace.

⁶ An oracle concerning the Beasts of Negeb:
    Through a land of hardship and vicissitude,
      of lions and the ᵃroaringᵃ king of beasts,
      of vipers and the fiery flying serpent,
    they carry their wealth
      on the backs of young asses,
    their riches on the humps of camels,
      to a people who cannot profit them.
⁷ Egypt's help shall be futile and vain;
    therefore I refer to her as an idle boast.

⁸ Go now, write on tablets concerning them;
    record it in a book for the last day,
    as a testimony forever.
⁹ They are a rebellious people,
    sons who break faith,
  children unwilling to obey
    the law of the Lord,
¹⁰ who say to the seers, See not!
    and to those with visions,
  Predict not what is right for us:
    flatter us; foresee a farce!
¹¹ Get out of the way;
    move aside, off the path!
  Cease confronting us
    with the Holy One of Israel!

a6   Heb. *mēhem, of them,* emended to *nôhēm*

¹² Therefore, thus says the Holy One of Israel:
Because you have rejected this word,
and rely on manipulation and double dealing,
and on them are dependent,
¹³ this iniquity will be to you
as a perilous breach exposed in a high wall
which suddenly and unexpectedly collapses.
¹⁴ It shall shatter with a crash
like an earthenware vessel
ruthlessly smashed,
among whose fragments
shall not be found a shard
with which to scoop lit embers
from a fireplace,
or dip water from a tank.

¹⁵ For thus says my Lord the Lord,
the Holy One of Israel:
By a calm response triumph;
with quiet confidence gain the victory.
But you would have none of it.
¹⁶ For you thought, Not so; we will flee on horses!
Therefore shall you flee indeed.
We will ride on swift mounts!
Therefore shall your pursuers be swifter.
¹⁷ You will flee by the thousand
at the threat of one,
by thousands at the threat of five,
till you are left
as a flagstaff on a mountaintop,
an ensign on a hill.

¹⁸ Then will the Lord delay *his coming*,
that he may favor you;
out of mercy toward you
he will remain aloof.
For the Lord is the God of justice;
blessed are all who wait for him.

¹⁹ O people of Zion, O inhabitants of Jerusalem,
    you shall have no cause to weep.
He will graciously respond
    at the cry of your voice;
he will answer you
    as soon as he hears it.
²⁰ Though my Lord give you the bread of adversity
    and the water of affliction,
yet shall your Teacher remain hidden no longer,
    but your eyes shall see the Master.
²¹ Your ears shall hear words from behind you
    saying, This is the way; walk in it!
    should you turn left or right.
²² You will discard as unclean
    your graven idols plated with silver,
    your cast idols gilded in gold;
you will eject them
    as a menstruous woman *her impurity*
    and say, Away with you!

²³ Then will he water with rain
    the seed you sow in the ground,
that the land's increase of food
    may be rich and abundant.
In that day your cattle shall graze
    in ample pasture lands,
²⁴ and the oxen and asses
    that till the soil
eat grain silage
    winnowed with shovel and fork.
²⁵ On all mountain heights and prominent hills
    shall appear streams of running water,
on the day of the great slaughter,
    when the towers fall.
²⁶ The light of the moon
    shall be as the light of the sun,
    and the light of the sun increase sevenfold;

as the light of seven days shall it be,
    in the day the Lord binds up
the fracture of his people
    and heals their open wound.

27 Behold, the Lord Omnipotent*b* coming from afar!
    His wrath is kindled, heavy is his grievance;
his lips flow with indignation,
    his tongue is like a devouring fire.
28 His breath is like a raging torrent
    that severs at the neck.
He comes to sift the nations
    in the sieve of falsehood;
with an erring bridle on their jaws
    he will try the peoples.
29 But for you there shall be singing,
    as on the night when a festival commences,
and rejoicing of heart, as when men march
    with flutes [and drums and lyres]*c*
on their way to the mountain of the Lord,
    to the Rock of Israel.
30 The Lord will cause his voice to resound,
    and make visible his arm
    descending in furious rage,
with flashes of devouring fire,
    explosive discharges and pounding hail.
31 At the voice of the Lord
    the Assyrians will be terror-stricken,
    they who used to strike with the rod.
32 At every sweep of the staff of authority,
    when the Lord lowers it upon them,
    they will be fought in mortal combat.
33 For Tophet has been prepared of old,
    a hearth indeed, made ready for rulers;
broad and deep is its fire pit
    and ample its pyre;

*b*27   Lit. *the name of the Lord*
*c*29   Terms brought up from verse 32, where they follow *they shall be fought,*
        a probable textual dislocation

the Lord's breath burns within it
    like a river of lava.

31 Woe to those who go down to Egypt for help,
    relying on horses,
putting their trust in immense numbers
    of chariots and vast forces of horsemen,
but who do not look to the Holy One of Israel,
    nor inquire of the Lord!

² Yet he too is shrewd
    and will bring disaster *upon them,*
    and not retract his words.
He will rise up against the brood of miscreants
    and allies of evildoers.
³ The Egyptians are human, not divine;
    their horses are flesh, not spirit:
when the Lord stretches out his hand,
    those who help them will stumble
    and those helped will fall;
both shall come to an end together.

⁴ For thus said the Lord to me:
    As a lion or a young lion growls over the prey
when the shepherds muster
    in full force against him,
and is not dismayed at the sound of their voice
    nor daunted by their numbers,
so shall the Lord of Hosts be when he descends
    to wage war upon Mount Zion
    and upon its heights.
⁵ As birds hover over [the nest],[a]
    so will the Lord of Hosts guard Jerusalem;
by protecting it he will deliver it,
    by passing over it, preserve it.

---

*a*5   Text emended to include direct object Heb. *qēn* before the similar sounding
adverb *kēn, so*

⁶ Return to him from whom you have contrived to go far astray, O children of Israel. ⁷ For in that day every one of you will despise your idolatrous silver and gold by which your hands have incurred guilt.

⁸ And Assyria shall fall by a sword not of man;
    a sword not of mortals shall devour them:
before that sword they shall waste away
    and their young men melt;
⁹ their captain*b* shall expire in terror
    and their officers shrink from the ensign,
says the Lord, whose fire is in Zion,
    whose furnace is in Jerusalem.

32 A king shall reign in righteousness
    and rulers rule with justice.
² And a man shall become as a shelter
    from the wind or refuge from the storm,
like brooks of water in a desert place,
    or the shade of a large rock in arid country.

³ The eyes of those who see shall not be shut,
    and the ears of those who hear shall listen.
⁴ The minds of the rash
    shall learn understanding,
and the tongues of the stammerers
    master eloquence.
⁵ The godless shall no longer be regarded as noble
    nor rogues considered respectable.
⁶ For the godless utter blasphemy;
    their heart ponders impiety:
how to practice hypocrisy and preach
    perverse things concerning the Lord,
leaving the hungry soul empty,
    depriving the thirsty *soul* of drink.
⁷ And rogues scheme by malevolent means
    and insidious devices to ruin the poor,

*b*9   Lit. *rock*, perhaps a military term

and with false slogans and accusations
   to denounce the needy.
⁸ But the noble are of noble intent,
   and stand up for what is virtuous.

⁹ Up, and listen to my voice, O complacent women;
   you careless daughters, hear my words!
¹⁰ In little more than a year
   you shall be in anguish, O carefree ones,
for when the harvest is over,
   the produce shall fail to arrive.
¹¹ Be alarmed, you complacent women;
   be perturbed, O careless daughters!
Strip yourselves bare;
   put sackcloth around your waists.
¹² Beat your breasts for the choice fields
   and flourishing vines,
¹³ for my people's land
   shall be overgrown with briars and thorns.
Mourn for all the amusement houses
   in the city of entertainment,
¹⁴ for the palaces shall lie abandoned,
   the clamorous towns deserted.
High rises and panoramic resorts
   shall become haunts for ever after,
the playground of wild animals,
   a browsing place for flocks.

¹⁹ᵃ For by a hail shall forests be felled,
   cities utterly leveled.
¹⁵ Then ᵇ shall a Spirit from on high
   be poured out on us;
the desert shall become productive land
   and lands now productive
   reckoned as brushwood.
¹⁶ So shall justice inhabit the desert,
   and righteousness abide in the farm land.

*a*19   Verse appears out of sequence in the text
*b*15   Heb. ʿad, until, emended to ʾaz

¹⁷ And the effect of justice shall be peace,
   and the result of righteousness
   an assured calm forever.
¹⁸ My people shall dwell in peaceful settlements,
   in safe neighborhoods,
   in comfortable dwellings.
²⁰ Blessed are you,
   who shall then sow by all waters,
   letting oxen and asses range free.

33 Woe to you, despoiler,
   who yourself was not despoiled;
O treacherous one,
   with whom none have been treacherous:
when you have done with devastating,
   you shall be devastated;
when you are through betraying,
   they shall betray you!

² O Lord, be favorable toward us;
   we have waited for thee.
Be our^a strength of arm
   from morning to morning,
   our salvation in troubled times.

³ The peoples fled from thy thunderous voice;
   at thine uprising the nations scattered.
⁴ Their spoil was harvested
   in the manner of caterpillars;
like insatiable locusts
   they rushed upon it.
⁵ But the Lord is supreme,
   for he dwells on high;
with justice and righteousness
   he will replenish Zion.
⁶ Your faithfulness in time *of trial*
   shall prove to be a strength,

*a*2   Heb. *their*

your wisdom and knowledge your salvation;
your fear of the Lord shall be your riches.

⁷ See, their stalwarts sob in public;
the champions of peace weep bitterly.
⁸ The highways are desolate,
travel is at an end.
The treaties have been violated,
their signatories*ᵇ* held in contempt;
man is disregarded.
⁹ The Land lies withered and forlorn,
Lebanon wilts shamefully;
Sharon has been turned into a dry waste,
Bashan and Carmel are denuded.

¹⁰ Now will I arise, says the Lord;
I will now become prominent,
now gain preeminence.
¹¹ You who conceived chaff
and brought forth stubble,
the fire of your own breath devours you!
¹² Whole nations have been burned like lime,
mown down like thorns and set ablaze.
¹³ Take heed what I have done,
you who are far off;
you who are near,
be apprised of my might!

¹⁴ The sinners in Zion are struck with fear;
the godless are in the grip of trembling:
Who among us can live
through the devouring fire?
Who among us can abide
eternal burning?
¹⁵ They who conduct themselves righteously
and are honest in word,
who disdain extortion
and stay their hand from taking bribes,

*b*8   So 1QIsaᵃ; MT reads *cities*

85

who stop their ears at the mention of murder,
  who shut their eyes at the sight of wickedness.
¹⁶ They shall dwell on high;
  the impregnable cliffs are their fortress.
Bread is provided them,
  their water is sure.

¹⁷ Your eyes shall behold the King in his glory
  and view the expanse of the earth.
¹⁸ You shall recount in your mind the terror:
  Where are those who conducted the census?
Where are those who levied the tax?
  Where are the ones who appraised the towers?
¹⁹ The insolent people are not to be seen,
  a nation of incomprehensible speech,
whose babbling tongue was unintelligible.

²⁰ Behold Zion, the city of our solemn assemblies;
  let your eyes rest upon Jerusalem,
the abode of peace—an immovable tent,
  whose stakes shall never be uprooted,
  nor any of its cords severed.
²⁴^cNone who reside there shall say, I am ill;
  the people who inhabit it
  shall be forgiven their iniquity.
²¹ May the Lord ^dcause us to dwell^d there,
  a country of rivers and broad streams,
where no warships sail
  or majestic fleets pass by.
²³^cTheir riggings hang loose;
  they hold not the mast in place
  nor spread out the sail.
Now shall spoil in abundance be divided,
  and even the lame take part in the plunder.
²² For the Lord is our Judge,
  and the Lord our Lawgiver.

c24, c23   Verse appears out of sequence in the text
d21   Heb. ʾaddîr, mighty one, emended to yādîr

The Lord is our King;
    he himself will save us.

34 Come near, you nations, and hear!
    Pay attention, you peoples!
Let the earth give heed,
    and all who are upon it,
    the world, and all who spring from it.
² The Lord's rage is upon all nations,
    his fury upon all their hosts;
he has doomed them,
    consigned them to the slaughter.
³ Their slain shall be flung out
    and their corpses emit a stench;
ᵃtheir blood shall dissolve on the mountains,
    ⁴ [their fat] decompose [on the hills]ᵃ—
when the heavens are rolled up as a scroll,
    and their starry hosts shed themselves
    with one accord,
like withered leaves from a vine,
    or shrivelled fruit from a fig tree.
⁵ When my sword drinks its fill in the heavens,
    it shall come down on Edom in judgment,
    on the people I have sentenced to damnation.

⁶ The Lord has a sword
    that shall engorge with blood
    and glut itself with fat—
the blood of lambs and he-goats,
    the kidney fat of rams.
For the Lord will hold a slaughter in Bozrah,
    an immense massacre in the land of Edom;

---

*a*3, *a*4   A problematic couplet, whose literal translation of MT reads *the moun-tains shall dissolve with their blood, and all the host of heaven decompose.* Heb. *kol ṣĕbāʾ haššāmayim,* emended to *gibʿôt mĕḥelbām* and the sense of the passage rendered congruous with its context; cf. the parallelism *blood/fat,* verses 6, 7, and the reading *hills* for *host of heaven.* LXX"

⁷among them shall fall bison, bulls, and steers.
    Their land shall be saturated with blood,
    their soil enriched with fat.
⁸For it is the Lord's day of vengeance,
    the year of retribution on behalf of Zion.

⁹*Edom's*ᵇ streams shall turn into lava
    and her earth into brimstone;
    her land shall become as burning pitch.
¹⁰Night and day it shall not be quenched;
    its smoke shall ascend forever.
It shall remain a wasteland
    from generation to generation;
    through endless ages none shall traverse it.
¹¹But hawks and falcons shall possess it,
    and owls and ravens inhabit it.
It shall be surveyed with muddled measure
    and chaotic weight.
¹²Shall they summon its nobles
    when it is no kingdom,
    when all its lords no longer exist?
¹³For thorns shall overgrow its palaces,
    thistles and briars its strongholds;
it shall become the haunt of howling creatures,
    a reserveᶜ for birds of prey.
¹⁴Prairie wolves shall greet jackals,
    and wild goats call to one another.
There too shall the night owl find repose
    and discover for herself a resting place.
¹⁵There shall the hawk owl nest and lay eggs,
    hatch them and brood over her young.
There too shall kites come together,
    each one accompanying her mate.

¹⁶Search, and read it in the book of the Lord:
    None is unaccounted for,
    not one lacks her mate.

*b*9   Heb. *Her*
*c*13   Heb. *ḥāṣîr, grass,* emended to *ḥāṣēr*

By his mouth he decreed it,
    by his Spirit he brings them together.
[17] It is he who allots them an inheritance,
    his hand that divides it by measure.
They shall possess it forever,
    inhabit it from generation to generation.

35

Wilderness and arid land shall be jubilant;
    the desert shall rejoice
    when it blossoms like the crocus.
[2] Joyously it shall break out in flower,
    singing with delight;
it shall be endowed with the glory of Lebanon,
    the splendor of Carmel and Sharon.
The glory of the Lord
    and the splendor of our God
they shall see *there*.

[3] Strengthen the hands grown feeble,
    steady the failing knees.
[4] Say to those with fearful hearts,
    Take courage, be unafraid.
See, your God is coming to avenge
    and to reward;
God himself will come and deliver you.

[5] Then shall the eyes of the blind be opened
    and the ears of the deaf unstopped.
[6] Then shall the lame leap like deer,
    and the tongue of the dumb shout for joy.
Water shall break forth in the wilderness
    and streams *flow* in the desert.
[7] The land of mirages shall become one of lakes,
    the thirsty place springs of water;
in the haunt of howling creatures
    [shall marshes break out],[a]
    in the reserves[b] shall come rushes and reeds.

a7   Heb. *ribṣâh, her resting place,* emended to *tiprōṣ biṣṣâ*
b7   Heb. *ḥāṣîr, grass,* emended to *ḥāṣēr; cf.* 34.13

⁸ There shall be highways and roads
  which shall be called the Way of Holiness,
ᶜfor they shall be for suchᶜ *as are holy.*
  The unclean shall not traverse them;
  on them shall no reprobates wander.
⁹ No lions ᵈshall be encountered there,ᵈ
  nor shall wild beasts intrude.
But the redeemed shall walk them,
  ¹⁰ the ransomed of the Lord shall return;
they shall come singing to Zion,
  their heads crowned with everlasting joy.
They shall have won joy and gladness
  when sorrow and sighing flee away.

36 In the fourteenth year of King Hezekiah's *reign,*
Sennacherib king of Assyria marched against all
the fortified cities of Judea and seized them. ² And the
king of Assyria sent Rabshakeh with a large army from
Lachish to King Hezekiah at Jerusalem. And he took up a
position by the aqueduct of the Upper Reservoir, on the
road to the Laundry Plaza. ³ And Eliakim the son of Hilkiah,
overseer of the palace, Shebna the secretary, and Joah the
son of Asaph, the record keeper, went out to him.

⁴ And Rabshakeh said to them, Please tell Hezekiah,
Thus says the great king, the king of Assyria: On what
grounds do you behave with such confidence? ⁵ Do you
suppose that in war mere words are *sufficient* tactics or
show of strength? In whom have you put your trust,
that you have rebelled against me? ⁶ It is clear you de-
pend on the support of Egypt, that splintered reed which
enters and pierces the palm of any man who leans on it.
Such is Pharoah king of Egypt to all who rely on him!
⁷ But if you tell me, We rely on the Lord our God, is he
not the one whose shrines and altars Hezekiah abolished,

c8   Phrase transposed; in text follows *traverse them*
d9   Text emended to replace Heb. *lōʾ yihyeh šām, shall not be there,* with *lōʾ yim-
       māṣēʾ šām,* which occurs as a duplication (fem.) following *intrude*

telling Judea and Jerusalem to worship *only* at this altar? ⁸Come now, wager with my lord the king of Assyria: I will give you two thousand horses, if you are able to put riders on them. ⁹How then shall you repulse even one of the least of my lord's servants, depending as you do on Egypt for chariots and horsemen? ¹⁰Moreover, could I have marched against this land and destroyed it without the Lord? For the Lord told me to come against this land and destroy it.

¹¹Then Eliakim, Shebna and Joah said to Rabshakeh, Please speak to your servants in Aramaic, which we understand. Do not speak to us in Judean in the ears of the people who are on the wall.

¹²But Rabshakeh replied, Did my lord send me to say these things to you and to your lord and not to the men sitting on the wall, who with you are to eat their own dung and drink their own urine?

¹³Then Rabshakeh stood and called out in a loud voice in Judean, Hear the words of the great king, the king of Assyria! ¹⁴Thus says the king: Do not let Hezekiah delude you! He cannot deliver you. ¹⁵Do not let Hezekiah make you trust in the Lord by saying, The Lord will surely save us; this city shall not be given into the hand of the king of Assyria.

¹⁶Do not listen to Hezekiah! Thus says the king of Assyria: Make peace with me by coming out to me. Then every one of you will eat from his own vine and his own fig tree and drink water from his own cistern, ¹⁷until I come back and take you to a land like your own, a land of grain and wine, a land of grain *fields* and vineyards.

¹⁸*Beware*, lest Hezekiah mislead you by saying, The Lord will save us. Were any gods of the nations able to save their lands out of the hand of the king of Assyria? ¹⁹Where are the gods of Hamath and Arpad? Where are the gods of Sepharvaim? Did they deliver Samaria out of my hand? ²⁰Who of all the gods of those countries saved his land from my hand, that the Lord should save Jerusalem from my hand?

²¹ But they remained silent, replying nothing, for the king had commanded them not to answer him.

²² Then Eliakim the son of Hilkiah, overseer of the palace, Shebna the secretary, and Joah the son of Asaph, the record keeper, went to Hezekiah with their clothes rent and reported to him the things Rabshakeh had said.

37 When King Hezekiah heard it, he rent his clothes and put on sackcloth and entered the house of the Lord. ² And he sent Eliakim the overseer of the palace, Shebna the secretary, and the elders of the priests in sackcloth to the prophet Isaiah the son of Amoz.

⁵ᵃ And when King Hezekiah's servants came to Isaiah, ³ they said to him, Thus says Hezekiah: This is a woeful day, a day of reproof and disgrace. Children have reached the point of birth, but there is no strength to deliver them. ⁴ It may be that the Lord your God has heard the words of Rabshakeh, whom his lord the king of Assyria has sent to scorn the living God, and will rebuke him for the things the Lord your God has heard, were you to offer up prayer on behalf of the remnant that is left.

⁶ And Isaiah said to them, Tell your lord, Thus says the Lord: Be not afraid because of the words with which you have heard the king of Assyria's subordinates ridicule me. ⁷ See, I will give him a notion to return home upon hearing a rumor, and will cause him to fall by a sword in his own land.

⁸ And when Rabshakeh heard that the king of Assyria had left Lachish, he withdrew and found him fighting against Libnah.

⁹ Now *Sennacherib*ᵇ received a report that Tirhakah king of Cush had set out to fight against him. And when he heard it, he sent messengers to Hezekiah, telling them, ¹⁰ Speak thus to Hezekiah king of Judah: Let not your god in whom you trust delude you into thinking that Jerusalem shall not

*a*5　Verse appears out of sequence in the text
*b*9　Heb. *he*

be given into the hand of the king of Assyria. ¹¹ You yourself have heard what the kings of Assyria have done, annex-
ing all lands. Shall you then escape? ¹² Did the gods of the
nations my fathers destroyed deliver them? *Did they deliver*
Gozan and Haran, Rezeph and the Edenites in Tel Assar?
¹³ Where are the kings of Hamath and Arpad and the kings
of the cities of Sepharvaim, Hena, and Ivvah?
¹⁴ And Hezekiah received the letter from the messengers
and read it. Then Hezekiah went up to the house of the
Lord and unrolled it before the Lord. ¹⁵ And Hezekiah
prayed to the Lord and said,
¹⁶ O Lord of Hosts, God of Israel, who sittest enthroned
between the cherubim, thou alone art God over all the
kingdoms of the earth. It is thou who madest the heavens
and the earth...
¹⁷ O Lord, give ear and hear; O Lord, open thine eyes and
see. Listen to all the words Sennacherib has sent to mock
the living God.
¹⁸ O Lord, the kings of Assyria have indeed destroyed all
peoples* and their lands, ¹⁹ committing their gods to the
fire. For they were no gods, but mere works of men's hands,
of wood and of stone, and so they could destroy them.
²⁰ But now, O Lord our God, deliver us out of his hand,
that all kingdoms on earth may know that thou alone
art Lord.
²¹ Then Isaiah the son of Amoz sent word to Hezekiah,
saying, Thus says the Lord, the God of Israel: Because you
have prayed to me concerning Sennacherib king of Assyria,
²² this is what the Lord has spoken against him:
> The Virgin Daughter of Zion
> holds you in contempt;
> she laughs you to scorn.
> The Daughter of Jerusalem
> shakes her head at you.
> ²³ Whom have you mocked and ridiculed?

---

*c*18   Heb. *hāʾărāṣôt, lands,* emended to *haggôyim;* cf. 2 Kings 19.17

      Against whom have you raised your voice,
    lifting your eyes to high heaven?
      Against the Holy One of Israel!
24 By your servants you have blasphemed the Lord.
      You thought, On account of my vast chariotry
    I have conquered the highest mountains,
      the farthest reaches of Lebanon.
    I have felled its tallest cedars,
      its choicest cypresses.
    I have reached its loftiest summit,
      it finest forest.
25 I have dug wells
      and drunk of foreign[d] waters.
    With the soles of my feet
      I have dried up all Egypt's rivers!

26 Have you not heard
      how I ordained this thing long ago,
    how in days of old I planned it?
      Now I have brought it to pass.
    You were destined to demolish fortified cities,
      turning them into heaps of rubble,
27 while their timorous inhabitants
      shrank away in confusion,
    becoming as wild grass, transiently green,
      or like weeds on a roof
  [e]that scorch[e] before they grow up.

28 But I know where you dwell,
      and your comings and goings,
      and how stirred up you are against me.
29 And because of your snortings
      and bellowings against me,
      which have mounted up to my ears,
    I will put my ring in your nose
      and my bit in your mouth
      and turn you back by the way you came.

d25 So 1QIsa[a]; 2 Kings 19.24. Term does not appear in MT
e27 So 1QIsa[a] *et al.*; MT reading obscure

³⁰ But to you this shall be a sign:
This year eat what grows wild,
and the following year
what springs up of itself.
But in the third year sow and harvest,
plant vineyards and eat their fruit:
³¹ the remnant of the house of Judah that survives
shall once more take root below
and bear fruit above.
³² For out of Jerusalem shall go a remnant,
and from Mount Zion a band of survivors.
The zeal of the Lord of Hosts will accomplish it.

³³ Therefore, thus says the Lord
concerning the king of Assyria:
He shall not enter this city
or shoot an arrow here.
He shall not advance against it with armor,
nor erect siegeworks against it.
³⁴ By the way he came he shall return;
he shall not enter this city, says the Lord.
³⁵ I will protect this city and save it,
for my own sake
and for the sake of my servant David.

³⁶ Then the angel of the Lord went out and slew a hundred and eighty-five thousand in the Assyrian camp. And when men arose in the morning, there lay all their dead bodies! ³⁷ So Sennacherib king of Assyria broke camp and withdrew. And he returned to Niniveh, where he dwelt. ³⁸ And as he was worshiping in the temple of Nisroch his god, his sons Adrammelech and Sharezer slew him with a sword and fled to the land of Ararat. And his son Esarhaddon succeeded him as king.

38 In those days Hezekiah became gravely ill. And the prophet Isaiah the son of Amoz came to him and said, Thus says the Lord: Put your house in order. You will die; you will not recover.

²At this Hezekiah turned his face toward the wall and prayed to the Lord: ³I beseech thee to remember, O Lord, how I have walked before thee faithfully and with full purpose of heart and have done what is good in thine eyes... And Hezekiah wept disconsolately.

⁴Then the word of the Lord came to Isaiah: ⁵Go and tell Hezekiah, Thus says the Lord, the God of your father David: I have heard your prayer and seen your tears. I will add fifteen years to your life. ⁶And I will deliver you and this city out of the hand of the king of Assyria; I will protect this city.

²¹ᵃAnd Isaiah gave instructions to take fig packs and apply them to the swelling so that he could recover.

²²ᵃBut Hezekiah said, What of a sign that I shall *again* go up to the house of the Lord?

⁷And Isaiah replied, This shall be a sign to you from the Lord, that the Lord will do the thing he has promised: ⁸See, I make the shadow cast by the afternoon sun on the dial of Ahaz recede the ten degrees it has gone down. So the sun reversed its descent by ten degrees on the dial.

⁹Hezekiah king of Judah's account of his illness, *written* upon his recovery:

> ¹⁰I said, in the prime of life
>> must I depart through Sheol's gates,
>> deprived of the balance of my years?
> ¹¹I thought, I shall not see ᵇthe Lordᵇ
>> in the land of the living;
> I shall not now behold Man
>> among those dwelling in mortality.
> ¹²My tabernacle is being uprooted,
>> carried away from me like a shepherd's tent.
> My life is cut off like woven fabric;
>> he is severing me from the loom.ᶜ

---

a21, a22   Verse appears out of sequence in the text
b11   Heb. *yāh yāh* emended to *yhwh*
c12   MT adds *as night has followed day, thou art bringing on my end!* (so vs. 13), a probable duplication. Cf. LXX

¹³ Can I contain myself until morning,
    while like a lion he racks my whole frame?
    Surely, as night has followed day,
      thou art bringing on my end!
¹⁴ Like a mounting lark I twitter,
    like a dove I murmur.
    My eyes are drawn looking heavenward;
      [I am utterly sleepless*d*
      from bitterness of soul...]*e*
    O Lord, I am in straits; be my surety!

¹⁵ But what shall I say
    when he has already spoken for me,
    when he himself has brought it about?
¹⁶ O my Lord, by means of such *trials*
    comes *a newness of* life,
    and throughout them all
      the renewal of my spirit.
¹⁷ Surely, for my own good
    I am in such dire distress;
    by its means thou drawest my soul
      out of the Pit of dissolution.
    For thou hast cast all my sins behind thee,
      [restoring and reviving me].*ʲ*
¹⁸ For Sheol cannot praise thee,
    nor Death glorify thee;
    those who go down into the Pit
      have no *further* hope of thy faithfulness.
¹⁹ But the living, only they bring thee praise,
    as I do this day;
    from father to sons they pass on
      the knowledge of thy faithfulness.

*d*14   Heb. *ʾeddaddeh kol šĕnôtai, I will wander all my years,* emended to *nôddĕdâ kol šĕnātî*
*e*14   Line brought up from verse 15, where it follows *brought it about*
*f*17   Phrase brought down from verse 16, where it follows *my spirit*

²⁰ O Lord, *may it please thee* to save me,
and we will perform music
all the days of our lives
in the house of the Lord.

39 At that time Merodach-Baladan the son of Baladan,
king of Babylon, sent letters and gifts to Hezekiah,
for he had heard of his illness and recovery. ²And
Hezekiah was glad of them and showed *the envoys*
his treasury—the silver and gold, the spices and fragrant
oils, and his entire armory and all that was in his treasuries. There was nothing in his palace or in all his realm
that Hezekiah did not show them.

³ Then the prophet Isaiah came to King Hezekiah and
said, What did those men say to you, and where did they
come from? And Hezekiah replied, They came from a
distant land; *they came* to me from Babylon. ⁴And
Isaiah asked, What did they see in your palace? And
Hezekiah said, They saw everything there is in my
palace. There is nothing in my treasuries that I did not
show them.

⁵ Then Isaiah said to Hezekiah, Hear the word of the Lord
of Hosts: ⁶The time shall come when everything in your
palace, and all that your forefathers have treasured up
until now, shall be carried away to Babylon. Nothing shall
be left, says the Lord. ⁷And from among your own sons,
your future offspring and descendants, they shall take *some*
to serve as eunuchs in the palace of the king of Babylon.

⁸ But Hezekiah said to Isaiah, The word of the Lord you
have spoken is good. For he thought, Then there shall be
peace and loyalty in my days.

40 Comfort and give solace to my people,
says your God;
²speak kindly to Jerusalem.
Announce to her that she has served her term,
that her guilt has been expiated.

She has received from the Lord's hand
    double for all her sins.

³ A voice calls out,
    In the desert prepare the way for the Lord;
  in the wilderness
    pave a straight highway for our God:
⁴ every ravine must be raised up,
    every mountain and hill made low;
  the uneven ground must become level
    and rough terrain a plain.
⁵ For the glory*ᵃ* of the Lord shall be revealed
    and all flesh see it at once.
  By his mouth the Lord has spoken it.

⁶ A voice said, Announce it.
    And I asked, How shall I announce it?
  All flesh is grass,
    and at its best like a blossom of the field.
⁷ᵇ Though the Spirit of the Lord breathe within it,
    the people themselves are but herbage—
⁸ grass that withers, flowers that fade—
    only the word of our God endures forever.

⁹ Scale the mountain heights,
    O Zion, herald of good tidings.
  Raise your voice mightily,
    O Jerusalem, messenger of good news.
  Make yourself heard, be not afraid;
    proclaim to the cities of Judah:
    Behold your God!
¹⁰ See, my Lord the Lord comes with power;
    his arm presides for him.
  His reward is with him;
    his work precedes him.

---

*a*5   Or, *presence*
*b*7   MT adds *Grass that withers, flowers that fade* (so vs. 8), a probable duplica-
    tion. Cf. 1QIsaᵃ; LXX

¹¹ Like a shepherd he pastures his flock:
  the lambs he gathers up with his arm
  and carries in his bosom;
 the ewes that give milk he leads gently along.

¹² Who measured out the waters
  with the hollow of his hand
 and gauged the heavens
  by the span of his fingers?
 Who compiled the earth's dust by measure,
  weighing mountains in scales,
  hills in a balance?
¹³ Who has comprehended the Spirit of the Lord,
  that a man should let him know his plan?
¹⁴ Of whom was he counselled
  that he might be enlightened,
 by whom instructed
  in the path of discretion,
 imparting to him knowledge,
  acquainting him with the way
  of understanding?

¹⁵ The nations are but drops from a bucket,
  counting no more than dust on a balance;
  the isles he displaces as mere specks.
¹⁶ Lebanon would not suffice to kindle a fire,
  nor *all* its beasts be adequate for sacrifice.
¹⁷ Before him all nations are as nothing;
  as less than the ether
  they are reckoned by him.

¹⁸ To whom then will you liken God?
  What does he resemble in your estimation?
¹⁹ A figure cast by the artisan,
  overlaid by the smith with gold,
 fitted with a silver chain
  from the craftsman?

^{41.7c}The artisan encourages the smith,
 and he who beats with a hammer
 urges him who pounds the anvil.
They say of the welding, It is good,
 though they fasten it with riveting
 that it may not come loose.
²⁰Those too poor for this *type of* sacrifice
 select a wood that resists decay.
They seek an expert sculptor
 to carve them an image
 that will not deteriorate.

²¹Are you so unaware,
 that you have not heard?
Have you not been told before,
 that you do not understand
 by whom the earth was founded?
²²—By him who sits enthroned
 above the earth's sphere,
to whom its inhabitants are as grasshoppers,
 who suspends the heavens like a canopy,
 stretching them out as a tent to dwell in.
²³By him who brings potentates to nought
 and makes the authorities of the world
 null and void:
²⁴when scarcely they are planted,
 or scarcely they are sown,
when hardly their stalk has taken root
 in the earth,
he puffs at them and they wither,
 and a storm sweeps them off as chaff.

²⁵To whom then will you liken me,
 to whom can I be compared?
 says the Holy One.
²⁶Lift your eyes heavenward and see:
 Who formed these?

*c*41.7 Verse appears out of sequence in the text

He who brings forth their hosts by number,
    calling each one by name.
Because he is almighty and all powerful,
    not one is unaccounted for.

[27] Why then do you say, O Jacob,
    and speak thus, O Israel:
Our path has become obscured from the Lord;
    our cause is overlooked by our God?
[28] Is it not known to you;
    have you not heard?
The Lord is the God of eternity,
    Creator of the ends of the earth.
He does not grow faint or weary;
    his intelligence cannot be fathomed.
[29] He supplies the weary with energy
    and increases in vigor
    those who lack strength.
[30] Youths grow faint and weary,
    and young men slump down *of exhaustion*.
[31] But they who hope in the Lord
    shall be renewed in strength:
they shall ascend as on eagles' wings;
    they shall run without wearying,
they shall walk and not faint.

41 Be silent before me, O isles;
    become still, you peoples!
Let them come forward and state their case;
    let us stand trial together.
[2] Who has raised up Righteousness from the east,
    calling him to *the place of* his foot?
Who has delivered nations to him,
    toppled their rulers,
rendering them as dust to his sword,
    as driven stubble to his bow?

³ He puts them to flight, passing on unhindered
    by paths his feet have never trod.
⁴ Who is at work accomplishing this,
    calling forth dynasties ahead of time?
  I, the Lord, first and last, am he.

⁵ The isles look on in fear;
    the ends of the earth are in trembling.
  They flock together*ᵃ* and come
    ⁶ to one another's aid,
    saying, each to his fellow, Courage!
⁸ But you, O Israel, my servant,
    Jacob, whom I have chosen,
    offspring of Abraham my beloved friend,
⁹ you whom I have taken
    from the ends of the earth,
    called from its farthest limits—
  to you I say, You are my servant;
    I have accepted you
    and not rejected you.
¹⁰ Be not fearful, for I am with you;
    be not dismayed, for I am your God.
  I will strengthen you; I will also succor you
    and uphold you with my righteous right hand.

¹¹ See, all who are enraged at you
    shall earn shame and disgrace;
  your adversaries shall come to nought,
    and perish.
¹² Should you look for those who contend with you,
    you shall not find them;
  whoever wars against you
    shall be reduced to nothing.
¹³ For I, the Lord your God,
    hold you by the right hand and say to you,
    Have no fear; I will help you.

*a*5   So 1QIsaᵃ; term lacking in MT

¹⁴Be not afraid, you worms of Jacob;
O men of Israel, [be not dismayed]:^b
I am your help, says the Lord;
your Redeemer is the Holy One of Israel.
¹⁵I will make of you
a sharp-toothed threshing sledge
of new design, full of spikes:
you shall thresh mountains to dust
and make chaff of hills.
¹⁶As you winnow them,
a wind shall take them away,
a tempest dispel them.
Then will you rejoice in the Lord
and glory in the Holy One of Israel.

¹⁷When the poor and needy require water,
and there is none,
and their tongue becomes parched
with thirst,
I the Lord will answer their want;
I, the God of Israel, will not forsake them.
¹⁸I will open up streams in barren hill country,
springs in the midst of the plains;
I will turn the desert into lakes,
parched lands into fountains of water.
¹⁹I will bring cedars and acacias,
myrtles and oleasters in the wilderness;
I will place cypresses,
elms and box trees in the steppes—
²⁰that all may see it and know,
consider it, and perceive
that the Lord's hand did this,
that the Holy One of Israel created it.

²¹Present your case, says the Lord;
submit your evidence, says the King of Jacob.

---

*b*14   Text reconstructed on basis of meter and parallelism; cf. verse 10

²² Let them come forward and recount to us
  their prophecies of events heretofore.
What were they? Tell us,
  that we may examine them
and know whether they were fulfilled.
  Or predict the future for us:
²³ Tell us of events to come hereafter,
  so that we may know you are gods.
Perform something good or evil
  at which we will be dazzled
and all stand in awe.
²⁴ It is clear you are of no account,
  that your works ^camount to nothing;^c
whoever accepts you is himself an abomination.

²⁵ I have raised up one from the north
  who calls on my name,
who shall come from the direction of sunrise.
  He shall come upon dignitaries as on mud,
tread them as clay like a potter.
²⁶ Who announced this beforehand,
  so we would know,
declared it ahead of time,
  that we might say, He was ^dright?^d
Indeed, not one could foretell it,
  not one make it known;
no one has heard from you
  any [prophetic]^e utterance.
²⁷ But to Zion, he shall be its harbinger;^f
  I will appoint him as a herald of tidings
to Jerusalem.

---

c24 Heb. ʾapaᶜ (unknown) emended to ʾāpes
d26 Lit. *The righteous one*, a pun on the subject of verses 2, 25
e26 Heb. riʾšôn, a probable corrupt form (cf. pl. riʾšônôt, vs. 22; mērʾōš, vs. 26),
  included in present verse; term commences verse 27 in MT
f27 Heb. hanōmeh (cf. Arab.); so 1QIsaᵃ. MT reads hinnām, *behold them/here*
  they are

²⁸ For when I looked there was no one,
 not one who could offer counsel,
or when I questioned them,
 who could answer a word.
²⁹ Surely they are all iniquitous,
 their works worthless;
their outpourings are but wind and emptiness.

42 My servant whom I sustain,
 my chosen one in whom I delight,
him I have endowed with my Spirit;
 he will dispense justice to the nations.*
² He will not shout or raise his voice
 to make himself heard in public.
³ Even a bruised reed he will not break;
 a dim wick he will not snuff out.
He will perform the work of justice
 in the cause of truth.
⁴ Neither shall he himself grow dim or be bruised
 till he has brought about justice in the earth.
The isles await his law.

⁵ Thus says the Lord God,
 who frames and suspends the heavens,
who gives form to the earth and its creatures,
 the breath of life to the people upon it,
 spirit to those who walk on it:
⁶ I the Lord have rightfully called you
 and will grasp you by the hand;
I have created you and appointed you
 to be a covenant for the people,
 a light to the nations,*
⁷ to open eyes that are blind,
 to free captives from confinement
and from prison those who sit in darkness.

*a*1, *a*6 Heb. *gôyîm,* also *Gentiles*

106

⁸I am the Lord; that is my name.
　I will not relinquish my glory to another,
　　nor praise to wrought idols.
⁹The prophecies of the former events
　　indeed came to pass,
　but new things I yet foretell.
　　Before they spring up I declare them to you.

¹⁰Sing to the Lord a new song;
　　sing his praise from the end of the earth.
ᵇLet the sea roar,ᵇ and all that lives in it,
　　the isles and they who inhabit them.
¹¹Let the desert and its cities raise *their voice*,
　　and the villages where Kedar dwells;
　let the inhabitants of Sela sing for joy
　　and cry out from the tops of the mountains.
¹²O let them give glory to the Lord,
　　and in the isles speak out in praise of him.
¹³The Lord will come forth like a warrior,
　　his passions aroused like a fighter;
　he will give the war cry,
　　raise the shout of victory over his enemies.
¹⁴For a long time I have been silent,
　　keeping still and restraining myself.
　But now I will scream like a woman in labor
　　and breathe hard and fast all at once.
¹⁵I will lay waste mountains and hills
　　and make all their vegetation wither;
　I will turn rivers into dry land
　　and evaporate lakes.
¹⁶Then will I lead the blind
　　by a way they did not know,
　　and guide them in paths unfamiliar;
　the darkness confronting them
　　I will turn into light,
　　and the uneven ground make level.
　These things I will not fail to perform.

ᵇ10　Heb. *yôrdê hayyām, they who go down to the sea,* emended to *yirʿam hayyām*

¹⁷ But those who trust in idols
>and esteem their images as gods
>shall retreat in utter confusion.
¹⁸ O you deaf, listen;
>O you blind, look and see!
¹⁹ Who is blind but my own servant,
>or so deaf as the messenger I have sent?
>Who is blind like those I have commissioned,
>as uncomprehending
>as the servant of the Lord—
²⁰ seeing much but not giving heed,
>with open ears hearing nothing?
²¹ It is the will of the Lord
>that for his righteousness' sake
>they magnify the law
>and become illustrious.
²² Instead, they are a people plundered and sacked,
>all of them trapped in holes,
>hidden away in dungeons.
>They have become a prey,
>yet no one rescues them,
>a spoil, yet none demands restitution.

²³ Who among you hearing this will take heed
>and be mindful of it hereafter?
²⁴ Who is it that hands Jacob over to plunder
>and Israel to despoilers, if not the Lord,
>against whom we have sinned?
>For they have no desire to walk in his ways
>or obey his law.
²⁵ So in the heat of his anger
>he pours out on them the violence of war,
>till it envelopes them in flames—
>yet they remain unaware—
>till it sets them on fire;
>yet they take it not to heart.

43 But now, thus says the Lord—
 he who formed you, O Jacob,
 he who created you, O Israel:
Do not fear, for I have redeemed you.
 I have called you by name; you are mine.
² When you cross the waters,
 I will be with you;
 when you traverse the rivers,
 you shall not be overwhelmed.
Though you walk through the fire,
 you shall not be burned;
 its flame shall not consume you.
³ For I the Lord am your God,
 I, the Holy One of Israel, am your Savior;
Egypt I have appointed as ransom for you,
 Cush and Seba *I give* in place of you.
⁴ Because you are precious
 and revered in my sight,
and because I love you,
 I give men in return for you,
peoples in exchange for your life.

⁵ Do not fear, for I am with you.
 I will bring your offspring from the east
 and gather you from the west;
⁶ I will say to the north, Give up!
 to the south, Withhold not!
 Bring my sons from afar
 and my daughters from the end of the earth—
⁷ all who are called by my name,
 whom I have formed, molded and wrought
 for my own glory.
⁸ Let go the people who are blind, yet have eyes,
 who are deaf, yet have ears.

⁹ When all nations unitedly assembled,
 when the peoples were gathered together,

who among them foretold these things,
    or predicted events that have come to pass?
Let them bring their witnesses
    and justify themselves,
    that those within hearing may say, It is true.
[10] But you are my witnesses, says the Lord,
    my servant whom I have chosen,
to the end that you may recognize it
    and believe me,
and perceive that I was the one
    who foretold them—
before me no god was formed,
    nor shall one exist after me.
[11] I myself am the Lord;
    apart from me there is no savior.
[12] It is I who foretold and wrought salvation,
    making it known
    when there was no strange god among you.
You are my witnesses, says the Lord,
    that I am divine,
[13] that from the first I have been present—
    from my hand none can deliver;
when I work, who can thwart it?

[14] Thus says the Lord, the Holy One of Israel,
    your Redeemer:
For your sake I launch *an attack* on Babylon
    and bring down as fugitives all the Chaldeans,
    they who sing the praises of shipping.
[15] I the Lord, your Holy One,
    Creator of Israel, am your King.
[16] Thus says the Lord—
    who provides a way in the Sea,
    a path through the mighty waters,
[17] who dispatches chariots and horses,
    armies of men in full strength;
they lie down as one, to rise no more,
    they flicker and die, snuffed out like a wick—

¹⁸ Never mind the prophecies of bygone events;
    do not dwell on things of the past.
¹⁹ See, I do a new thing; it is now springing up.
    Surely, you are aware of it:
  I am making roads through the desert,
    streams in the wasteland.
²⁰ The wild beasts do me honor,
    the jackals and birds of prey,
  for bringing water to the wilderness,
    streams to the dry land,
  that I may give drink to my chosen people,
    ²¹ the people I formed for myself
  to speak out in praise of me.

²² But you do not call upon me, O Jacob;
    you have grown weary of me, O Israel.
²³ Yet *I required* not that you bring me
    offerings from your flocks
  or pay me homage by sacrificial slaughter;
  I have not burdened you with oblations
    or wearied you with burning incense.
²⁴ *Nor have I burdened you* to buy me
    the fragrant calamus
  or sate me with the fat of immolations.
  Yet you have burdened me with your sins,
    wearied me with your iniquities.
²⁵ But it is I myself, and for my own sake,
    who blot out your offenses,
    remembering your sins no more.
²⁶ Recount for me *the past*;
    let us plead each our case.
    Speak up and vindicate yourself.
²⁷ Your first father transgressed;
    your spokesmen sinned against me.
²⁸ Therefore I let *ªthe holy cities*ª be profaned;
    I gave Jacob to be ostracised,
    Israel to execration.

a28   Heb. *śārê qōdeš, the princes of the sanctuary,* emended to *ʿārê qōdeš;* cf. 47.6;
     64.10

44 Hear now, Jacob my servant,
and Israel whom I have chosen.
² Thus says the Lord, your Maker,
who formed you from the womb
and succored you:
Be not afraid, O Jacob, my servant,
and Jeshurun whom I have chosen.
³ I will pour water on the thirsty *soil*,
showers upon the dry ground;
I will pour out my Spirit upon your offspring,
my blessing on your posterity.
⁴They shall shoot up like grass
among streams*ᵃ* of water,
like willows by running brooks.
⁵ One will say, I am the Lord's,
and another name himself Jacob.
Yet others will inscribe on their arm,
To the Lord,
and adopt the name Israel.

⁶Thus says the Lord, the King of Israel,
the Lord of Hosts, their Redeemer:
I was at the first and I am at the last;
apart from me there is no God.
⁷ Who predicts *ᵇwhat happensᵇ* as do I,
and is the equal of me
in appointing a people from of old *ᶜas types,ᶜ*
foretelling things to come?
⁸ Be not perturbed or shaken.
Have I not made it known to you from of old?
Did I not foretell it,
you being my witnesses?
Is there a God, then, apart from me?
There is no Rock unknown to me.

---

*a*4　So LXX; word lacking in MT
*b*7　Heb. *yiqrāʾ, will call,* emended to *yiqrâ*
*c*7　Heb. *wĕʾōtîyôt, the coming things,* emended to *kĕʾōtôt;* cf. 8.18; 1QIsaᵃ, 45.11

⁹ All who manufacture idols are deranged;
    the things they cherish profit nothing.
  Those who promote them
    are themselves sightless and mindless,
    to their own dismay.
¹⁰ Who would fashion a god or cast an idol
    that cannot benefit them?
¹¹ Their whole society is confused;
    their fabricators are mere mortals.
  Were they all to assemble
    and take their stand *before me,*
  they would at once cringe in fear.

¹² The smith with his tools
    works the iron over the coals
  and gives it shape by hammering;
    he forges his *god* by the strength of his arm:
  when he becomes hungry,
    he no longer has strength;
  if he fails to drink water,
    he begins to grow faint.
¹³ The woodworker draws a diagram,
    sketching his *idol* with a marker.
  He creates it by chiselling
    to the outline of the dividers;
  he gives it a human likeness,
    resembling man's beauty,
    fit to lodge in a house.
¹⁴ He is required to cut down cedars;
    he must select holms and oaks
  and care for them
    among the trees of the forest.
  He plants firs, which the rain makes grow:
¹⁵ that which serves men as fuel,
    which they use to warm themselves
  or light fire with to bake bread,
    of that they create gods which they adore,
    from it they make idols to which they stoop.

¹⁶ Half of it they burn in the fire.
  ^dOver it they broil a roast;^d
they eat the meat and are satisfied.
    They also warm themselves and say,
    Ah, it is warm ^ein front of^e the fire!
¹⁷ From the rest they make a god, their idol,
    to which they bow in adoration and pray,
    Save us; you are our god!
¹⁸ They have become unaware and insensible;
    their eyes are glazed so they cannot see,
    their minds are incapable of discernment.
¹⁹ They reflect not,
    nor have the sense or comprehension to say,
  Part of this I burned in the fire;
    I also baked bread in its embers,
    roasted meat and ate it.
  Am I not making an abomination of what is left?
    Do I not stoop to a mere lump of wood?
²⁰ They are followers of ashes;
    their deluded minds have distracted them.
  They cannot liberate themselves *from them*
    or say,
  Surely this thing in my hand is a fraud.

²¹ Ponder these things, O Jacob,
    and you,^f O Israel,
    for you are my servant.
  I have created you to be my servant, O Israel;
    do not disregard me.
²² I have removed your offenses like a thick fog,
    your sins like a cloud of mist.
  Return to me; I have redeemed you.
²³ Sing, O heavens, for what the Lord has done;
    cause it to resound, O earth beneath!

Burst into song, O mountains,
  forests, and all trees therein:
the Lord has redeemed Jacob;
  he shall be glorified in Israel.

²⁴ Thus says the Lord, your Redeemer,
  who formed you from the womb:
I am the Lord, the Maker of all things,
  who alone suspends the heavens,
  who himself gives form to the earth,
²⁵ who annuls the predictions of imposters
  and makes fools of diviners,
who turns wise men about
  and makes nonsense of their knowledge,
²⁶ who fulfills the word of his servant,
  accomplishes the aims of his messengers,
who says of Jerusalem,
  It shall be reinhabited,
and of the cities of Judah,
  They shall be rebuilt,
  their ruins I will restore,
²⁷ who says to the deep, Become dry;
  I am drying up your currents,
²⁸ who says of Cyrus, He is my shepherd;
  he will do whatever I will.
He will say of Jerusalem that it must be rebuilt,
  its temple foundations relaid.

45

Thus says the Lord to his anointed,
  to Cyrus, whom I grasp by the right hand,
to subdue nations before him,
  to ungird the loins of rulers,
opening doors ahead of him,
  letting no gates remain shut:
² I will go before you
  and level all obstacles;
I will break in pieces brazen doors
  and cut through iron bars.

115

³I will give you hidden treasures
and secret hoards of wealth—
that you may know that it is I the Lord,
the God of Israel, who calls you by name.
⁴For the sake of my servant Jacob,
and Israel my chosen,
I call you by name—
I named you when yet you knew me not—
⁵I am the Lord, there is none other;
apart from me there is no God.
I girded you up when yet you knew me not—
⁶that men from where the sun rises
to where it sets
may know that without me there is nothing,
that I am the Lord,
and that there is none other.
⁷I fashion light and form darkness;
I occasion peace and cause calamity.
I, the Lord, do all these things.
⁸Rain down from above, O heavens;
let the skies overflow with righteousness.
Let the earth receive it
and salvation *blossom;*
let righteousness spring up forthwith.
I, the Lord, create it.

⁹Woe to those in conflict with their Maker,
mere shards of earthenware pottery!
As though the clay were to say
to him who molds it,
What are you doing?
Your hands have no skill for the work!
¹⁰Woe to those who say to their Father,
What have you begotten?
or to the Woman,
What have you borne?

*a*8   So 1QIsaᵃ; LXX; MT reads *they bear fruit*

¹¹ Thus says the Lord,
    the Holy One of Israel, their Maker:
  Will you ask me*b* for signs*c*
  concerning my children,
  or dictate to me
  about the deeds of my hands?
¹² It is I who made the earth
    and created man upon it;
  I with my hand*d* suspended the heavens,
  appointing all their host.
¹³ It is I who rightfully raise him up,
  who facilitate his every step;
  he will rebuild my city and set free my exiles
  without price or bribe, says the Lord of Hosts.

¹⁴ Thus says the Lord:
  The wealth of Egypt and merchandise of Cush
  *e*shall pass on to you and become yours,*e*
  as shall the Sabeans, a people tall in stature.
  They shall walk behind you in chains
  and bow down to you, entreating you,
  Surely God is in you; no other gods exist!

¹⁵ Truly thou art a God who dissembles himself,
  O Savior, God of Israel.

¹⁶ As one the makers of inventions
  retired in disgrace,
  utterly dismayed and embarrassed.
¹⁷ But Israel is saved by the Lord
  with an everlasting salvation;
  you shall not be dismayed or put to shame
  worlds without end.

---

*b*11   Heb. *šĕʾălûnî, Ask me,* emended to *tišʾalûnî*
*c*11   So 1QIsa*ᵃ*; cf. 7.11. MT reads Heb. *ʾōtiyôt, the coming things*
*d*12   So LXX; MT vocalization is plural. Cf. 48.13
*e*14   Phrase transposed; in text follows *tall in stature*

¹⁸ For thus says the Lord who created the heavens,
    the God who formed the earth—
who made it secure and organized it,
    not to remain a chaotic waste,
but designed it to be inhabited—
    I am the Lord, there is none other.
¹⁹ I speak not in secret
    from some place in a land of darkness;
I have not asked Jacob's offspring
    to seek me amid chaos.
I the Lord tell righteousness,
    and am forthright of speech.

²⁰ Gather yourselves and come;
    draw near, all you fugitives of the nations.
They who carried about their wooden idols
    and prayed to gods that could not save them
    were caught unawares.
²¹ Speak up and present your case;
    go ahead and consult one another.
Who foretold these things of old,
    predicted them long ago?
Did not I, the Lord,
    apart from whom there is no God?
Did not I, the God of righteousness,
    except for whom there is no Savior?

²² Turn to me and save yourselves,
    all you ends of the earth;
    I am God, there is none other.
²³ By myself I swear it—
    righteousness has issued from my mouth,
    by a decree that cannot be revoked:
To me every knee shall bow
    and every tongue swear *allegiance.*
²⁴ It shall be said of me,
    By the Lord alone come vindication and might.

Before him must come in shame
 all who were incensed against him.
25 In the Lord shall all Israel's offspring
 justify themselves and have cause to boast.

46 Bel slumps down, Nebo is stooped over:
 their idols are *loaded* upon beasts and cattle;
 the images you bore aloft
 are piled as burdens on weary animals.
2 *Such gods*^a altogether sag and bow down,
 unable to rescue their burden;
 they themselves go into captivity.

3 Hear me, O house of Jacob,
 and all you remnant of the house of Israel,
 who have been a load on me since birth,
 borne up by me from the womb:
4 Even to your old age, I am present;
 till you turn grey, it is I who sustain you.
 It is I who made you, and I who bear you up;
 it is I who carry and rescue you.

5 To whom will you compare me
 or count me equal?
 To whom will you liken me,
 that we should appear similar?
6 They who squander gold from the purse
 and weigh out silver on the scales
 hire a smith to make them a god
 they can bow down to and worship.
7 They bear it aloft,
 carrying it on their shoulders;
 when they set it in position, there it stands,
 unable to budge from its place.
 Though they cry to it for help,
 it does not answer;
 it cannot save them from trouble.

a2 Heb. *they*

⁸Put yourselves in mind of this
and come to your senses;
take it to heart, you offenders.
⁹Review the prophecies of the events of old!
I am God, there is none other.
I am divine;
nothing resembles me.
¹⁰I foretell the end from the beginning,
from ancient times,
things not yet done.
I speak, and my purposes take effect;
I accomplish all my will.
¹¹I summon a bird of prey from the east,
from a distant land
the man I have foreordained.
What I have spoken, I bring to pass;
what I have planned, I do.
¹²Hear me, you stubborn-hearted,
who are far from righteousness:
¹³I have brought near my righteousness;
it is not now far off—
my salvation shall no longer be delayed.
I will grant deliverance in Zion,
and to Israel my glory.

47   Get down and sit in the dust,
O Virgin Daughter of Babylon;
squat on the ground, dethroned,
O Daughter of the Chaldeans.
You shall no more be spoken of
as delicate and refined.
²Take two grindstones and grind flour;
unveil, disrobe, bare your legs,
wade through streams:
³your nakedness shall be exposed
and your shame uncovered.

I will take vengeance
and not be entreated of men,
[4] *says* our Redeemer, the Holy One of Israel,
whose name is the Lord of Hosts.

[5] Sit speechless; retire into obscurity,
O Daughter of the Chaldeans.
No longer shall you be called,
Mistress of Kingdoms.
[6] I was provoked by my people,
so I let my inheritance be defiled.
I gave them into your hand,
and you showed them no mercy;
even the aged you weighed down heavily
with your yoke.
[7] You thought, I, the Eternal Mistress,
exist forever!
and did not consider these,[a]
or remember her[b] final destiny.

[8] Now therefore hear this, O pampered lady,
securely enthroned, thinking to herself,
I exist, and other than me there is nothing;
I shall not be widowed
or bereaved of children:
[9] Bereavement and widowhood
shall suddenly overtake you, both in one day.
They shall come upon you in full,
notwithstanding your many magical feats
and exceedingly strong combinations.

[10] Secure in your wickedness,
you thought, No one discerns me.
By your skill and science you were led astray,
thinking to yourself, I exist,
and there is none besides me!

a7   Viz., the redeemed descendants of those who went into captivity; cf. verse 4
b7   Viz., Zion's; cf. 52.1-3

¹¹ Catastrophe shall overtake you,
 which you shall not know how
 ^cto avert by bribes;^c
disaster shall befall you
 from which you cannot ransom yourself:
there shall come upon you sudden ruin
 such as you have not imagined.

¹² Persist, then, with your combinations
 and with your many magical feats,
at which you have exerted yourself
 since your youth.
It may still be of use to you;
 perhaps you can hinder^d it.
¹³ But you are powerless,
 despite all your tactics.
Now let those who unravel the heavens,
 who observe the stars
and make predictions month by month,
 stand by you and save you!
¹⁴ See, as stubble they are burnt up
 in the fire,
unable themselves to escape
 the force^e of the flame.
These are no embers to warm anyone;
 such is no fire to sit by!
¹⁵ This is what your procurers^f
 have profited you—
those for whom you have exerted yourself
 since your youth;
each deviates his own way,
 none is there to save you.

---

c 11 Heb. *šaḥrāh* (obscure) emended to *saḥdāh*; contrast Israel to this verse, 43.3; 45.13

d 12 Heb. *taʿărôṣî, cause terror,* emended to *taʿăṣôrî*; cf. 66.9

e 14 Lit. *hand*

f 15 Or, *merchants.* Noun transposed; in text follows *exerted yourself.* Cf. verse 12

48 Hear this, O house of Jacob,
    you who are named Israel—
though you*ᵃ* stem from the lineage*ᵇ* of Judah—
    who take oaths in the name of the Lord
and invoke the God of Israel—
    though not in truth or in righteousness—
² who call yourselves of the holy city,
    upheld by the God of Israel,
    whose name is the Lord of Hosts:
³ The prophecies of the events of the past
    I made known long beforehand;
no sooner did they issue from my mouth,
    than I caused them to be announced.
Then, suddenly I acted
    and they came about.
⁴ For I knew how stubborn you were—
    your neck was an iron sinew,
    your brow was brazen—
⁵ therefore I told you them beforehand;
    I announced them to you
    before they transpired,
lest you should say, My idols did it;
    my graven and wrought images caused it!

⁶ But you have heard *ᶜ*the whole vision;*ᶜ*
    how is it you do not proclaim it?
Yet as of now, I announce to you new things,
    things withheld and unknown to you,
⁷ things now coming into being, not hitherto,
    things you have not heard of before,
    lest you should say, Indeed I knew them!
⁸ You have not heard them,
    nor have you known them;

*a*1   Heb. *they*
*b*1   Lit. *loins.* Heb. *mimmê, from the waters,* emended to *mimmĕʿê;* cf. the term
      in verse 19
*c*6   Heb. *ḥazēh kullāh, See all of it!* emended to *ḥāzût kullāh;* cf. 29.11

before this your ears
    have not been open to them.
For I knew you would turn treacherous;
    you were called
    a transgressor from the womb.
⁹For my own name's sake
    I have bridled my wrath;
on account of my renown
    I have shown restraint toward you
    by not entirely destroying you.
¹⁰See, I am refining you,
        though not as silver;
    I am testing*d* you
        in the crucible of affliction.
¹¹For my own sake, on my own account, I do it,
        that my name*e* be not dishonored,
    nor my glory, which I give to no other.

¹²Hear me, O Jacob, and Israel, my elect:
        I am he who was at the first,
        and I am he who is at the last.
¹³It was my hand that founded the earth,
        my right hand that stretched out the heavens;
        when I call them, they arise at once.
¹⁴All of you, assemble and hear:
        Who among you*ᶠ* foretold these things?
    It is him the Lord loves,
        who shall perform his will in Babylon;
        his arm shall be against the Chaldeans.
¹⁵I myself have spoken it
        and also called him;
    I have brought him,
        and I will prosper*ᵍ* his way.

---

*d*10 So 1QIsaᵃ; MT reads *choosing*
*e*11 So LXX; noun lacking in MT
*f*14 Heb. *bāhem, among them,* emended to *bākem*
*g*15 So LXX; MT reads *and he shall prosper*

¹⁶ Come near me and hear this:
    I have not made predictions in secret;
at their coming to pass,
    I have been present.
Now my Lord the Lord has sent me;
    his Spirit *is in me.*^h

¹⁷ Thus says the Lord, the Holy One of Israel,
    your Redeemer:
I the Lord your God instruct you to your good,
    guiding you in the way you should go.
¹⁸ Had you but obeyed my commandments,
    your peace would have been as a river,
    your righteousness like the waves of the sea;
¹⁹ your offspring would have been
    as the sands in number,
    your descendants as many as their grains.
Their names would not have been cut off
    and obliterated from my presence.

²⁰ Go forth out of Babylon, flee from Chaldea!
    Make this announcement
    with resounding voice;
broadcast it to the end of the earth.
    Say, The Lord has redeemed his servant Jacob.
²¹ They thirsted not when he led them
    through arid places:
he caused water to flow for them
    from the rock;
he cleaved the rock and water gushed out.

²² But there is no peace, says the Lord,
    for the wicked.

49 Hear me, O isles; listen, you distant peoples:
    The Lord called me before I was in the belly;
before I was in my mother's womb,
    he mentioned me by name.

*h*16   Cf. 63.11

²He has made my mouth like a sharp sword—
  in the shadow*a* of his hand he hid me.
He has made me into a polished arrow—
  in his quiver he kept me secret.
³He said to me, You are my servant,
  Israel, in whom I will be glorified.
⁴I had thought, I have labored in vain,
  I have spent my strength for nothing
  and to no purpose!
Yet my cause rested with the Lord,
  my recompense with my God.

⁵For now has said the Lord—
  he who formed me from the womb
  to be his servant,
to restore Jacob to him,
  Israel having been gathered to him;
for I won honor in the eyes of the Lord
  when my God became my strength—
⁶he said: It is too small a thing
  for you to be my servant
to raise up the tribes of Jacob
  and to restore those preserved of Israel.
I will also appoint you
  to be a light to the nations,*b*
that my salvation
  may be to the end of the earth.

⁷Thus says the Lord,
  the Redeemer and Holy One of Israel,
to him who is despised as a person,
  who is abhorred by his nation,
  a servant to those in authority:
Rulers shall rise up when they see you,
  heads of state shall prostrate themselves,
because the Lord keeps faith with you,
  because the Holy One of Israel has chosen you.

*a*2   Also, *guise*
*b*6   Also, *Gentiles;* cf. verse 22; 42.1, 6

⁸Thus says the Lord:
At a favorable time I have answered you;
in the day of salvation
I have come to your aid:
I have created you, and I appoint you
to be a covenant of the people,
to restore the Land
and reapportion the desolate estates,
⁹to say to the captives, Come forth!
and to those in darkness, Show yourselves!
They shall feed along the way
and find pasture on all barren heights;
¹⁰they shall not hunger or thirst,
nor be smitten by oppressive heat or by the sun:
he who has mercy on them will guide them;
he will lead them by springs of water.
¹¹All my mountain ranges I will appoint as roads;
my highways shall be on high.
¹²See these, coming from afar,
these, from the northwest,
and these, from the land of Sinim.
¹³Shout for joy, O heavens; celebrate, O earth!
Burst into song, O mountains!
The Lord is comforting his people,
showing compassion for his afflicted.

¹⁴But Zion said, The Lord has forsaken me,
my Lord has forgotten me.
¹⁵Can a woman forget her suckling infant,
or feel no compassion
for the child of her womb?
Although these shall forget,
I will not forget you.
¹⁶See, I have engraved you on my palms;
ᶜI have sealed youᶜ
to be continually before me.

---

c16   Heb. *ḥômōtayik, your walls,* emended to *ḥātamtîk*

127

¹⁷ Your sons shall hasten your ravagers away—
   those who ruined you shall depart from you.
¹⁸ Lift up your eyes and look around you;
   with one accord they gather and come to you.
As surely as I live, says the Lord,
   you shall adorn yourself with them all
   as with jewels,
bind them on you as does a bride.

¹⁹ For your ruins and ravaged places
   and your land laid waste
shall now be too small for your inhabitants,
   notwithstanding the departure
   of your devourers.
²⁰ The children born
   during the time of your bereavement
shall yet say in your ears,
   This place is too cramped for us;
   give us space in which to settle!
²¹ And you will say to yourself,
   Who bore me these
   while I was bereaved and barren?
I was exiled, banished;
   by whom were these reared?
When I was left to myself,
   where were they?

²² Thus says my Lord the Lord:
   I will lift up my hand to the nations,
   raise my ensign to the peoples;
and they will bring your sons in their bosoms
   and carry your daughters on their shoulders.
²³ Kings shall be your foster fathers,
   queens your nursing mothers.
They will bow down before you,
   their faces to the ground;
   they will lick the dust of your feet.

Then you shall know that I am the Lord,
    and that they who hope in me
    are not disappointed.

24 Can the warrior's spoil be taken from him,
    or the tyrant's*d* captives escape free?
25 Yet thus says the Lord: The warrior's spoil*e*
    shall indeed be taken from him,
  and the tyrant's captives*f* escape free:
    I myself will contend with your contenders,
    and I will deliver your children.
26 I will feed your oppressors with their own flesh;
    they shall be drunk with their own blood
    as with wine.
And all flesh shall know that I the Lord
    am your Savior,
that your Redeemer is the Valiant One of Jacob.

50

Thus says the Lord:
    Where is your mother's bill of divorce
    with which I cast her out?
Or to which of my creditors did I sell you?
    Surely, by sinning you sold yourselves;
because of your crimes
    was your mother an outcast.
2 Why was no one there when I came;
    why did no one answer when I called?
Was my hand too short to redeem you;
    have I no power to deliver?
By a mere rebuke I dry up the Sea;
    rivers I turn into desert—
their fish become parched*a* for lack of water
    and perish because of thirst.

*d*24   So 1QIsa*a*; LXX. MT reads *ṣaddîq, the righteous one's*
*e*25   So 1QIsa*a*; MT reads *captives*
*f*25   So 1QIsa*a*; MT reads *spoil*
*a*2   So 1QIsa*a*; LXX. MT reads *turn foul*

³ I clothe the heavens
    with the blackness of mourning;
I put up sackcloth to cover them.

⁴ My Lord the Lord has endowed me
    with a learned tongue,
that I may know how to preach
    to those grown weary a word to waken them.
  Morning by morning he wakens my ear to hear,
    as at study;
⁵ my Lord the Lord has opened my ear,
    and I rebel not, nor back away:
⁶ I offered my back to smiters,
    my cheeks to those who plucked out the beard;
I hid not my face from insult and spitting.
⁷ Because my Lord the Lord helps me,
    I shall not be disgraced;
I have set my face like flint,
    knowing I shall not be confounded.
⁸ He who vindicates me is near me.
  Who has a dispute with me?
Let us face one another!
  Who will bring charges against me?
Let him confront me with them!
⁹ See, my Lord the Lord sustains me.
  Who then will incriminate me?
Surely all such shall wear out like a garment;
    the moth shall consume them.

¹⁰ Who among you fears the Lord
    and heeds the voice of his servant,
who, though he walk in darkness
    and have no light,
trusts in the name of the Lord
    and relies on his God?
¹¹ But you are lighters of fires, all of you,
    who illuminate*ᵇ* with mere sparks.

*b*11 Heb. *mèʾazrê, gird up,* emended to *mèʾîrê*

Walk then by the light of your fires
  and by the sparks you have kindled.
This shall you have from my hand:
  you shall lie down in agony.

51 Hear me, you followers of righteousness,
  seekers of the Lord:
Look to the rock from which you were cut,
  to the quarry out of which you were hewn;
²look to Abraham your father,
  to Sarah who bore you.
He was but one when I called him,
  but I blessed him by making him numerous.
³For the Lord is comforting Zion,
  bringing solace to all her ruins;
he is making her wilderness like Eden,
  her desert as the garden of the Lord.
Joyful rejoicing takes place there,
  thanksgiving with the voice of song.

⁴Listen to me, my people;
  give heed to me, O my nation:
The law shall go forth from me;
  my precepts shall be a light to the peoples.
  Then, suddenly I will act:
⁵My righteousness shall be at hand
  and my salvation proceed;
my arms shall judge the peoples—
  the isles anticipate me, awaiting my arm.
⁶Lift up your eyes to the heavens;
  look on the earth beneath:
the heavens shall vanish as by smoke,
  the earth wear out like a garment—
its inhabitants shall die
  in the manner of vermin.
But my salvation shall be everlasting;
  my righteousness shall never fail.

⁷Hear me, you who know righteousness,
    O people in whose heart is my law:
Do not fear the reproach of men;
    be undaunted by their ridicule.
⁸For the moth shall consume them
    like a garment;
moths shall devour them like wool.
    But my righteousness shall endure forever,
my salvation through endless generations.

⁹Awake, arise; clothe yourself with power,
    O arm of the Lord!
Bestir yourself, as in ancient times,
    as in generations of old.
Was it not you who carved up Rahab,
    you who slew the dragon?
¹⁰Was it not you who dried up the Sea,
    the waters of the mighty deep,
and made of ocean depths a way
    by which the redeemed might pass?
¹¹Let the ransomed of the Lord return!
    Let them come singing to Zion,
their heads crowned with everlasting joy;
    let them obtain joy and gladness,
and sorrow and sighing flee away.

¹²I myself am your Comforter.
    Who are you that you fear mortal man,
the children of men
    who shall be turned to grass?
¹³Have you forgotten the Lord, your Maker—
    who suspends the heavens,
    who sets the earth in place—
that you go all day in constant dread
    of the oppressor's rage
as he readies himself to wreak destruction?
    What is there to the wrath of the oppressor?

¹⁴ Soon now shall he who is bowed down
  be set free;
 he shall not die *as those destined* for the Pit,
  neither shall he want for food.
¹⁵ It is I the Lord your God,
  whose name is the Lord of Hosts,
  who stir up the Sea so that its waves roar.
¹⁶ I will put my words in your mouth
  and shelter you in the shadow of my hand,
 while I replant the heavens
  and set the earth in place,
 that I may say to Zion, You are my people.

¹⁷ Rouse yourself; awaken and rise up, O Jerusalem,
  you who have drunk from the Lord's hand
 the cup of his wrath,
  drinking to the dregs the bowl of stupor.
¹⁸ There was none to guide her *home*
  among all the children she bore,
 none to take her by the hand
  of all the sons she reared.
¹⁹ Twofold *calamity* has befallen you:
  desolation, ruin—and who laments you?
  famine, the sword—and who consoles*^a* you?
²⁰ Your children lie in a faint
  at the corner of every street,
  taken in a net like bison.
 They have their fill of the wrath of the Lord,
  of your God's angry rebuke.

²¹ Now therefore hear this, O wretched one,
  drunk, though not with wine.
²² Thus says the Lord, your Lord and God,
  who defends the cause of his people:
 I am taking the cup of stupor from your hand;
  you shall drink no more
  from the bowl of my wrath.

*a*19   So 1QIsa*ᵃ*; LXX. MT reads *how can I console*

²³ And I give it into the hand of your tormentors,
    those who said of your life,
Lie prostrate that we may go over you—
    so that you made your back as the ground,
a mere thoroughfare to passers-by.

52   Awake, arise; clothe yourself with power,
        O Zion!
Put on your robes of glory,
    O Jerusalem, holy city.
No more shall the uncircumcised and defiled
    enter you.
² Shake yourself free, rise from the dust;
    sit enthroned, O Jerusalem.
Loose yourself from the bands around your neck,
    O captive Daughter of Zion.
³ Thus says the Lord:
    You were sold without price,
and you shall be redeemed without money.

⁴ For thus says my Lord the Lord:
    At first my people went down to Egypt
    to sojourn there.
Then the Assyrians subjugated them for nothing.
⁵ And now, what have I here? says the Lord.
    My people are taken over without price;
    those who preside over them
      ᵃact presumptuously,ᵃ says the Lord,
and my name is constantly in abuse
    all the day.
⁶ Therefore shall my people
    come to know my name;
in that day *they shall know*
    that I, who speak, am at hand.
⁷ *Then shall they say,*
    How comely upon the mountains
    are the feet of the messenger announcing peace,

*a*5   Also, *mock*; so 1QIsaᵃ. MT reads *wail*

who brings tidings of good,
who heralds salvation,
saying to Zion, Your God reigns!

⁸ Hark! Your watchmen lift up their voice;
as one they cry out for joy:
before their very eyes they see
the Lord's return to Zion.
¹⁰ᵇ The Lord has bared his holy arm
in the eyes of all nations,
that all ends of the earth may see
our God's salvation.
⁹ Break out all together into song,
you ruined places of Jerusalem:
the Lord has comforted his people,
he has redeemed Jerusalem.

¹¹ Turn away, depart;
touch nothing defiled as you leave *Babylon.*ᶜ
Come out of her and be pure,
you who bear the Lord's vessels.
¹² But you shall not leave in haste or go in flight:
the Lord will go before you,
the God of Israel behind you.

¹³ My servant, being astute, shall be highly exalted;
he shall become exceedingly eminent:
¹⁴ just as heᵈ appalled many—
his appearance was marred
beyond human likeness,
his semblance unlike that of men—
¹⁵ so shall he yet astoundᵉ many nations,
rulers shutting their mouths at him—
what was not told them, they shall see;
what they had not heard, they shall consider.

*b*10 Verse transposed; in text appears out of sequence
*c*11 Heb. *there*
*d*14 Heb. *you*
*e*15 Or, *startle;* also *purge, sprinkle*

53   Who has believed our revelation?
        On whose account has the arm of the Lord
        been revealed?
² Like a sapling he grew up in his presence,
        a stalk out of arid ground.
    He had no distinguished appearance,
        that we should notice him;
    he had no *pleasing* aspect,
        that we should find him attractive.
³ He was despised and disdained by men,
        a man of grief, accustomed to suffering.
    As one from whom men hide their faces
        he was shunned, deemed by us of no merit.

⁴ Yet he bore our sufferings,
        endured our griefs,
    though we thought him stricken,
        smitten of God, and humbled.
⁵ But he was pierced for our transgressions,
        crushed because of our iniquities;
    the price of our peace he incurred,
        and with his wounds we are healed.
⁶ We all like sheep had gone astray,
        each of us headed his own way;
    the Lord brought together upon him
        the iniquity of us all.

⁷ He was harassed, yet submissive,
        and opened not his mouth—
    like a lamb led to slaughter,
        like a sheep, dumb before its shearers,
        he opened not his mouth.
⁸ By arrest and trial he was taken away.
        Who can apprise his generation
    that he was cut off from the land of the living
        for the crime of my people,
        to whom the blow was due?

⁹He was appointed among the wicked in death,ᵃ
    among the rich was his burial;ᵇ
yet he had done no violence,
    and deceit was not in his mouth.
¹⁰But the Lord willed to crush him,
    causing him suffering,
that, if heᶜ made his life an offering for guilt,
    he might see his offspring
    and prolong his days,
and that the purposes of the Lord
    might prosper in his hand.

¹¹He shall see the toil of his soul
    and be satisfied;
because of his knowledge,
    and by bearing their iniquities,
shall my servant, the righteous one,
    vindicate many.
¹²I will assign him an inheritance among the great,
    and he shall divide the spoil with the mighty,
because he poured out his soul unto death,
    and was numbered with criminals—
he bore the sins of many,
    and made intercession for the transgressors.

54 Sing, O barren woman who did not give birth;
        break into jubilant song,
you who were not in labor.
    The children of the deserted wife
shall outnumber those of the espoused,
    says the Lord.

²Expand the site of your tent;
    extend the canopies of your dwellings.
Do not hold back; lengthen your cords
    and strengthen your stakes.

ᵃ9, ᵇ9   Terms transposed; in text appear reversed. Cf. 14.20, and the lack of a
         burial for the wicked and violent Tyrant
ᶜ10   Heb. *you*

³ For you shall spread abroad
    to the right and to the left;
  your offspring shall dispossess the nations
    and resettle the desolate cities.

⁴ Be not fearful,
    for you shall not be confounded;
  be not ashamed,
    for you shall not be disgraced.
  You shall forget the shame of your youth
    and remember no more
    the reproach of your widowhood.
⁵ For he who espouses you is your Maker,
    whose name is the Lord of Hosts;
  he who redeems you is the Holy One of Israel,
    who is called the God of all the earth.
⁶ The Lord calls you back
    as a spouse forsaken and forlorn,
  a wife married in youth only to be rejected,
    says your God.
⁷ I forsook you indeed momentarily,
    but with loving compassion
    I will gather you up.
⁸ In a fleeting surge of anger
    I hid my face from you,
  but with everlasting charity
    I will have compassion on you,
  says the Lord, who redeems you.

⁹ This is to me as in the days*ᵃ* of Noah,
    when I swore that the waters of Noah
    would no more flood the earth.
  So I swear to have no more anger toward you,
    never again to rebuke you.
¹⁰ For the mountain shall be removed
    and the hills collapse with shaking,

*a*9   So 1QIsaᵃ; MT reads *waters*

but my charity toward you
>   shall never be removed,
> nor my covenant of peace be shaken,
>   says the Lord,
>   who has compassion on you.

¹¹ Poor wretch, tempest-tossed and disconsolate!
>   I will lay antimony for your building stones
>   and sapphires for your foundations;
¹² I will make your skylights of jacinth,
>   your gates of carbuncle,
>   and your entire boundary of precious stones.
¹³ All your children
>   shall be taught by the Lord,
> and great shall be the peace
>   of your posterity.
¹⁴ You shall be firmly established
>   through righteousness;
> you will be far from oppression
>   and have no cause to fear,
> far from ruin, for it shall not approach you.

¹⁵ Those who gather into mobs are not of me;
>   whoever masses against you
>   shall fall because of you.
¹⁶ It is I who create the smith
>   who fans the flaming coals,
> forging weapons to suit his purpose;
>   it is I who create the ravager to destroy.
¹⁷ Whatever weapon is devised against you,
>   it shall not succeed;
> every tongue that rises to accuse you,
>   you shall refute.
> This is the heritage of the servants of the Lord,
>   and such is their vindication*b* by me,
>   says the Lord.

b17   Or, *righteousness;* cf. verse 14

55

Attention, all who thirst;
  come for water!
You who have no money,
  come and buy food, that you may eat.
Come, buy wine and milk
  with no money and at no cost.
² Why do you spend money on what is not bread,
  your labor on what does not satisfy?
Hear me well:
  Eat what is good,
and your souls shall enjoy abundance.

³ Give ear and come unto me;
  pay heed, that your souls may live!
And I will make with you
  an everlasting covenant:
  my loving fidelity toward David.
⁴ See, I have appointed him
  a witness to the nations,
  a prince and lawgiver of the peoples.
⁵ You will summon a nation
  that was unfamiliar to you;
and a people to whom you were unfamiliar
  will hasten to you—
because of the Lord your God,
  the Holy One of Israel,
who gloriously endows you.

⁶ Inquire of the Lord while he is present;
  call upon him while he is near.
⁷ Let the wicked forsake their ways
  and sinful men their thoughts.
Let them return to the Lord,
  and he will have mercy on them;
to our God, who graciously pardons.

⁸ For my thought are not your thoughts,
  nor are your ways my ways, says the Lord.

⁹But as the heavens are higher than the earth,
    so are my ways higher than your ways
    and my thoughts *higher* than your thoughts.
¹⁰And as the rains and snows
    descend from the sky,
  and return not to it
    without watering the earth,
  to render it fertile and fruitful—
    providing seed for the sower
    and food for the eater—
¹¹so is the word that leaves my mouth:
    it does not return to me empty;
  it accomplishes what I desire,
    and achieves the purpose for which I sent it.

¹²You shall depart in joy
    and be led back in peace;
  the mountains and hills shall sing
    at your presence
  and the trees of the meadows
    all clap their hands.
¹³In place of the thornbush
    shall come up the cypress,
    in place of nettles the myrtle.
  This shall serve as a testimony of the Lord,
    an everlasting sign
  which shall not be done away.

56

Thus says the Lord:
    Observe justice and perform righteousness,
for soon my salvation will come
    and my righteousness be revealed.
²Blessed is the man who does so—
    the person who holds fast to them—
who keeps the Sabbath without profaning it,
    who stays his hand from doing any evil.

³ Let not the foreigner
   who adheres to the Lord say,
The Lord will surely exclude me from his people.
   And let not the eunuch say,
I am but a barren tree.
⁴ For thus says the Lord:
   As for the eunuchs who keep my Sabbaths
and choose to do what I will—
   holding fast to my covenant—
⁵ to them I will give a handclasp and a name
   within the walls of my house
   that is better than sons and daughters;
I will endow them with an everlasting name
   that shall not be cut off.
⁶ And the foreigners who adhere to the Lord
   to serve him,
who love the name of the Lord,
   that they may be his servants—
all who keep the Sabbath without profaning it,
   holding fast to my covenant—
⁷ these I will bring to my holy mountain
   and gladden in my house of prayer.
Their offerings and sacrifices
   shall be accepted on my altar,
for my house shall be known
   as a house of prayer for all nations.
⁸ Thus says my Lord the Lord,
   who gathers up the outcasts of Israel:
I will gather others to those already gathered.

⁹ All you wild beasts, you animals of the forest,
   come and devour!
¹⁰ Their watchmen are altogether blind
   and unaware;
all of them are but dumb watchdogs
   unable to bark,
   lolling seers fond of slumber.

¹¹ Gluttonous dogs, and insatiable:
    such indeed are insensible shepherds;
they are all diverted to their own way,
    every one after his own advantage.
¹² Come, *they say,* let us get wine
    and have our fill of liquor.
For tomorrow will be like today,
    only far better!

57 The righteous*ᵃ* disappear,
        and no man gives it a thought;
    the godly are gathered out,
        but no one perceives
    that from impending calamity
        the righteous*ᵃ* are withdrawn.
²They who walk uprightly shall attain to peace
        and shall rest in their beds.

³As for you, come here,
        you children of the sorceress,
        offspring of adulterer and harlot!
⁴At whose expense do you amuse yourselves?
    At whom do you open wide the mouth
    and stick out the tongue?
        Surely you are born of sin, a spurious brood,
⁵who burn with lust among the oaks,
        under every burgeoning tree,
    slayers of children in the gullies
        under the crags of rocks.
⁶Among the slippery stones of the ravines
        shall be your fate;
        they indeed are your lot.
    To them you pour out libations
        and make offerings.
    How shall I be appeased of such things?

---

*a*1   Or, *righteous one*

⁷ On a lofty mountain
   you have made prominent your bed,
      and there you ascend to offer sacrifices.
⁸ Behind doors and facades
   you have put up your emblems,
and have exposed yourself to *others* than I:
   mounting your bed,
you have laid it wide open.
   And you bargain with those
with whom you love to lie,
   your hand on their nakedness.*^b*
⁹ You bathe*^c* in oil for the king
   and increase your perfumes;
you send your solicitors far abroad
   and debase yourself to the depths.*^d*
¹⁰ Though wearied by your excessive ways,
   you have not admitted despair;
you have found livelihood,
   and have therefore not slackened.

¹¹ Yet on whose account
   are you uneasy and apprehensive,
that you pretend
   and do not mention me,
      nor even give me a thought?
Is it because I have so long kept silent
   that you no longer fear me?
¹² But I will expose your 'righteousness'
   and the wantonness of your exploits.
¹³ When you cry out in distress,
   let those who flock to you save you!
A wind shall carry all of them off;
   a vapor shall take them away.

---

*b*8   Lit. *foreparts*
*c*9   From Heb. root šārâ
*d*9   Heb. *Sheol*

But they who seek refuge in me
    shall possess the earth
and receive an inheritance
    in my holy mountain.
¹⁴ It will be said: Excavate, pave a road!
    Prepare the way;
remove the obstacles from the path of my people!

¹⁵ Thus says he who is highly exalted,
    who abides forever,
    whose name is sacred:
I dwell on high in the holy place,
    and with him who is humble
    and lowly in spirit—
refreshing the spirits of the lowly,
    reviving the hearts of the humble.
¹⁶ I will not contend forever,
    nor always be angry;
the spirits and souls I have made
    would faint before me.
¹⁷ By his sin of covetousness I was provoked;
    I struck him and hid *my face* in anger
when he strayed by following
    the ways of his heart.
¹⁸ Yet I have seen his conduct
    and will recover him;
I will guide him and amply console him
    and those who mourn him,
¹⁹ who partake^e of the fruit of the lips:
    Peace, wellbeing, to those far off
and to those who are near,
    says the Lord who heals him.
²⁰ But the wicked are like the raging Sea,
    unable to rest,
    whose waters heave up mire and mud:
²¹ there is no peace, says my God, for the wicked.

e19   Heb. *bôrēʾ, create,* emended to *bôrē*

145

58 Proclaim it aloud without restraint;
raise your voice like a trumpet!
Declare to my people their transgressions,
to the house of Jacob its sins.
² Yet they importune me daily,
eager to learn my ways,
like a nation practicing righteousness
and not forsaking the precepts of its God.

They inquire of me
concerning correct ordinances,
desiring to draw nearer to God:
³ Why, when we fast, do you not notice?
We afflict our bodies
and you remain indifferent!
It is because on your fastday
you pursue your own ends
and constrain all who toil for you.
⁴ You fast amid strife and contention,
striking out savagely with the fist.
Your present fasts are not such
as to make your voice heard on high.
⁵ Is this the manner of fasting I have required,
just a time for men to torment themselves?
Is it only for bowing one's head like a reed
and making one's bed of sackcloth and ashes?
Do you call that a fast,
a day of the Lord's good graces?

⁶ Is not this the fast I require:
To release from wrongful bondage,
to untie the harness of the yoke,
to set the oppressed at liberty
and abolish all forms of subjection?
⁷ Is it not to share your food with the hungry,
to bring home the wretchedly poor,
and when you see men underclad to clothe them,
and not to neglect your own kin?

⁸ Then shall your light break through
    like the dawn
and your healing speedily appear;
    your righteousness will go before you,
and the glory*a* of the Lord
    will be your rear guard.

⁹ Then, should you call, the Lord will respond;
    should you cry, he will say, I am here.
Indeed, if you will banish servitude
    from among you
    and the pointing finger and offensive speech,
¹⁰ if you will give of your own to the hungry
    and satisfy the needs of the oppressed,
then shall your light dawn amid darkness
    and your twilight become as the noonday.
¹¹ The Lord will direct you continually;
    he will satisfy your needs in the dearth
    and bring vigor to your limbs.
And you will become like a well-watered garden,
    like a spring of unfailing waters.
¹² They who came out of you
    will rebuild the ancient ruins;
you will restore the foundations
    of generations ago.
You shall be called a rebuilder of fallen walls,
    a restorer of streets for resettlement.

¹³ If you will keep your feet
    from *trampling* the Sabbath—
from achieving your own ends on my holy day—
and consider the Sabbath a delight,
    the holy *day* of the Lord venerable,
and if you will honor it
    by refraining from your everyday pursuits—
from occupying yourselves with your own affairs
    and speaking of *business* matters—

*a*8 Or, *presence*

¹⁴then shall you delight in the Lord,
>
> and I will make you traverse the heights
> of the earth
>
> and nourish you with
>
> the heritage of Jacob your father.
>
> By his mouth the Lord has spoken it.

59

Surely the Lord's hand
>
> has not become too short to save,
>
> nor his ear dull of hearing!
>
> ²It is your iniquities
>
> that separate you from your God;
>
> your sins hide his face,
>
> so that he does not hear you.

³For your palms are defiled with blood,
>
> your fingers with iniquity;
>
> your lips speak guile,
>
> your tongue utters duplicity.
>
> ⁴None calls for righteousness;
>
> no one sues for an honest cause.
>
> They rely on empty words,
>
> deceitfully spoken;
>
> they conceive misdeeds,
>
> they beget wickedness.
>
> ⁵They hatch vipers' eggs
>
> and spin spiders' webs;
>
> whoever eats of their eggs dies,
>
> and if any is smashed,
>
> there emerges a serpent.
>
> ⁶Their cobwebs are useless as clothing;
>
> their fabrications are worthless
> for covering themselves.
>
> Their works consist of wrongdoing;
>
> they manipulate injurious dealings.
>
> ⁷Their feet rush after evil;
>
> they hasten to shed innocent blood.

Their thoughts are preoccupied with mischief;
   havoc and disaster follow in their wake.
8 They are unacquainted with the way
  of perfection;
  integrity is not within their bounds.
   They have made crooked their paths;
  none who treads them knows peace.

9 Therefore redress remains far from us
   and righteousness is unable to reach us.
  We look for light,
   but there prevails darkness;
  for a glimmer *of hope,*
   but we walk amid gloom.
10 We grope along the borders like the blind;
   we flounder like those without eyes.
  We stumble at noon as in the dark of night;
   in the prime of life we resemble the dead.
11 We grumble like bears, all of us;
   we moan incessantly like doves.
  We expect justice when there is none;
   we look for salvation, but it eludes us.
12 For our transgressions before thee
   have multiplied;
   our sins testify against us.
  Our offenses are evident;
   we perceive our iniquities:
13 willfully denying the Lord,
   backing away from following our God,
  perversely planning ways of extortion,
   conceiving in the mind and pondering
   illicit transactions.
14 And so redress is compelled to back away,
   and righteousness to stand at a distance;
  truth stumbles in the public place
   and uprightness cannot enter.
15 When integrity is lacking,
   they who shun evil become a prey.

> The Lord saw that there was no justice,
>> and it displeased him.
> [16] When he saw it,
>> he wondered why there was no one,
> not one who would intervene.
>
> So his own arm brought about salvation for him;
>> his righteousness rallied to his cause.
> [17] He put on righteousness as a breastplate
>> and made salvation the helmet on his head;
> he clothed himself with vengeance for a garment
>> and wrapped himself in fury as in a robe.
> [18] According to what they deserve,
>> he will repay them:
> wrath upon his adversaries,
>> reprisals upon his enemies;
> to the isles he will render retribution.
>
> [19] From the west men will fear
>> the Lord Omnipotent,[a]
> and from the rising of the sun
>> his glory.[b]
> For he will come *upon them*
>> like a hostile torrent
>> impelled by the Spirit of the Lord.
> [20] But he will come as Redeemer to Zion,
>> to those of Jacob who repent of transgression,
> says the Lord.

[21] As for me, this is my covenant with them, says the Lord:
My Spirit which is upon you and my words which I have
placed in your mouth shall not depart from your mouth,
nor from the mouth of your offspring, nor from the mouth
of their offspring, says the Lord, from now on and forever.

*a*19 Lit. *the name of the Lord*
*b*19 Or, *presence*

60
Arise, shine, your light has dawned;
the glory of the Lord has risen upon you!
² Although darkness covers the earth,
and a thick mist the peoples,
upon you the Lord will shine;
over you his glory shall be visible.

³ Nations will come to your light,
their rulers to the brightness of your dawn.
⁴ Lift up your eyes and look about you!
They have all assembled to come to you:
your sons shall arrive from afar;
your daughters shall return to your side.
⁵ Then, when you see it, your face will light up,
your heart swell with awe:
the multitude of the Sea shall resort to you;
a host of nations shall enter you.
⁶ A myriad of camels shall cover *your land,ᵃ*
the dromedaries of Midian and Ephah;
all from Sheba will come,
bearing gold and frankincense
and heralding the praises of the Lord.
⁷ All Kedar's flocks will gather to you,
the rams of Nebaioth will serve you;
they shall be accepted as offerings on my altar,
and thus I will make glorious
my house of glory.

⁸ Who are these, aloft like clouds,
flying as doves to their portals?
⁹ From the isles they are gathering to me,
the ships of Tarshish in the lead,
to bring back your children from afar,
and with them their silver and gold,
to the Lord Omnipotent,ᵇ your God,
to the Holy One of Israel,
who has made you illustrious.

*a*6   Heb. *you*
*b*9   Lit. *the name of the Lord*

¹⁰ Foreigners will rebuild your walls,
   and their rulers will minister to you.
Though I struck you in anger,
   I will gladly show you mercy.
¹¹ Your gates shall always remain open;
   they shall not be shut day or night,
that a host of nations may be brought to you
   and their rulers escorted in.
¹² And the nation or kingdom
   that will not serve you shall perish;
such nations shall be utterly ruined.

¹³ The splendor of Lebanon shall become yours—
   cypresses, pines and firs together—
to beautify the site of my sanctuary,
   to make glorious the place of my feet.
¹⁴ The sons of those who tormented you
   will come bowing before you;
all who reviled you
   will prostrate themselves at your feet.
They will call you The City of the Lord,
   Zion of the Holy One of Israel.
¹⁵ Although you had been forsaken and abhorred,
   with none passing through *your land*,
yet I will make you an everlasting pride,
   the joy of generation after generation.
¹⁶ You will suck the milk of the nations,
   suckling at the breasts of rulers.
Then shall you know that I, the Lord,
   am your Savior,
that your Redeemer
   is the Valiant One of Jacob.
¹⁷ In place of copper I will bring gold,
   in place of iron, silver;
in place of wood I will bring copper,
   in place of stones, iron.
I will make peace your rulers
   and righteousness your oppressors:

¹⁸ tyranny shall no more be heard of in your land,
    nor dispossession or disaster
    within your borders;
  you will regard salvation as your walls
    and homage as your gates.

¹⁹ No longer shall the sun be your light by day,
    nor the brightness of the moon
    your illumination[c] at night:
  the Lord will be your everlasting light
    and your God your radiant glory.
²⁰ Your sun shall set no more,
    nor your moon wane:
  to you the Lord shall be an endless light,
    when your days of mourning are fulfilled.
²¹ Your entire people shall be righteous;
    they shall inherit the earth forever—
  they are the branch I have planted,
    the work of my hands, in which I am glorified.
²² The least of them shall become a clan,
    the youngest a mighty nation.
  I the Lord will hasten it in its time.

61

The Spirit of my Lord the Lord is upon me,
    for the Lord has anointed me
  to announce good tidings to the lowly;
    he has sent me to bind up the brokenhearted,
  to proclaim liberty to the captives
    and the opening of the eyes to the bound,
² to herald the year of the Lord's favor
    and the day of vengeance of our God,
    to comfort all who mourn:
³ to endow those who mourn in Zion,
    bestowing upon them a priestly headpiece
    in place of ashes,
  the festal anointing
    in place of mourning,

c19 So 1QIsa^a; LXX; noun lacking in MT

a resplendent robe
in place of a downcast spirit.
They shall be called oaks of righteousness
planted by the Lord for his glory.

4 They will rebuild the ancient ruins,
raise up the old waste places;
they will renew the desolate cities
demolished generations ago.
5 Aliens will tend and pasture your flocks;
foreigners will be your farmhands
and vinedressers.
6 But you shall be called
the priests of the Lord
and referred to as the ministers of our God.
You shall feed on the wealth of the nations,
and be gratified with their choicest provision.
7 Because their*a* shame was twofold,
and shouted insults were their lot,
therefore in their land
shall their inheritance be twofold,
and everlasting joy be theirs.

8 For I the Lord love just dealings—
but I abhor extortion in *those who* sacrifice—
and I will appoint them a sure reward;
I will make with them an eternal covenant.
9 Their offspring shall be renowned
among the nations,
their posterity in the midst of the peoples;
all who see them will acknowledge
that they are of the lineage the Lord has blessed.

10 I rejoice exceedingly in the Lord;
my soul delights in my God.
For he clothes me in garments of salvation;
he arrays me in a robe of righteousness—

*a*7   Heb. *your*

154

 like a bridegroom dressed in priestly attire,
  or a bride adorned with her jewels.
¹¹ For as the earth brings forth its vegetation,
  and as a garden causes what is sown
  to spring up in it,
 so will my Lord the Lord
  cause righteousness and praise to spring up
 in the presence of all nations.

62

 For Zion's sake I will not keep silent;
  for Jerusalem's sake I will not remain still
 till her righteousness shines like a light,
  her salvation like a flaming torch.
² The nations shall behold your righteousness,
  and all their rulers your glory;
 you shall be called by a new name,
  conferred by the mouth of the Lord.

³ Then shall you be a crown of glory
  in the hand of the Lord,
 a royal diadem
  in the palm of your God.
⁴ You shall no more be called the forsaken one
  nor your land referred to as desolate;
 you shall be known as her in whom I delight,
  and your land considered espoused.
 For the Lord shall delight in you
  and your land be espoused.
⁵ As a young man weds a virgin,
  so shall your sons wed you;
 as the bridegroom rejoices over the bride,
  so shall your God rejoice over you.

⁶ I have appointed watchmen on your walls,
  O Jerusalem,
 who shall not be silent day or night.
 You who call upon the Lord, let not up
  ⁷ nor give him respite

155

till he reestablishes Jerusalem
and makes it renowned in the earth.

8 The Lord has sworn by his right hand,
his mighty arm:
I will no more let your grain
be food for your enemies,
nor shall foreigners drink the new wine
you have toiled for.
9 Those who harvest it shall eat it,
giving praise to the Lord;
those who gather it shall drink it
within the environs of my sanctuary.

10 Pass on, go through gates;
prepare the way for the people!
Excavate, pave a highway cleared of stones;
raise the ensign to the nations!
11 The Lord has made proclamation
to the end of the earth:
Tell the Daughter of Zion,
See, your Salvation comes,
his reward with him,
his work preceding him.
12 They shall be called the holy people,
the redeemed of the Lord;
and you shall be known as in demand,
a city never deserted.

63   Who is this coming from Edom
in red-stained garments?
Who is this from Bozrah, arrayed in majesty,
pressing forward in the strength of his power?
It is I, who am mighty to save,
announcing righteousness!
2 Why are you clothed in red,
your garments like those who tread *grapes*
in the winepress?

3 Alone I have trodden out a vatful;
    of the nations no one was with me.
I trod them down in my anger;
    in my wrath I trampled them.
Their lifeblood spattered my garments,
    and I have stained my whole attire.

4 For I had resolved on a day of vengeance,
    and the year of my redeemed had come.

5 I glanced around, but none would lend help;
    I glared, but no one would assist.
So my own arm brought about salvation for me,
    and my wrath, it assisted me.
6 I trod nations underfoot in my anger;
    I made them drunk by my rage
when I cast their glory to the ground.

7 I will recount in praise of the Lord
    the Lord's loving favors,
according to all that the Lord has done for us,
    according to the great kindness
he has mercifully and most graciously
    rendered the house of Israel.
8 For he thought,
    Surely they are my people,
sons who will not play false;
    and so he became their Savior:
9 with all their troubles he troubled himself,
    the angel of his presence delivering them.
In his love and compassion
    he himself redeemed them;
he lifted them up and carried them
    all the days of old.
10 Yet they rebelled and grieved his holy Spirit,
    till he became their enemy
and himself fought against them.

¹¹ Then his people*^a* recalled the days
of Moses of old:*^b*
Where is he who brought them up out of the Sea
with the shepherd of his flock?
Where is he who put into him
his holy Spirit,
¹² who made his glorious arm proceed
at the right hand of Moses,
who divided the waters before them,
making an everlasting name for himself
¹³ when he led them through the deep?
Like the horse of the desert,
they stumbled not;
¹⁴ like cattle descending *the slopes of* ravines,
it was the Spirit of the Lord
that guided them.*^c*
So thou didst lead thy people, *O Lord*,
acquiring illustrious renown.

¹⁵ O look down from heaven,
from thy holy and glorious celestial abode,
and behold!
Where now are thy zeal and thy might?
The yearnings of thy bosom and thy compassion
are withheld from us!
¹⁶ Surely thou art our Father!
Though Abraham does not know us
or Israel recognize us,
thou, O Lord, art our Father;
Our Redeemer from Eternity is thy name.
¹⁷ Why, O Lord, hast thou made us stray
from thy ways,
hardening our hearts
so that we do not fear thee?

---

*a*11   Term transposed; in text follows *Moses*
*b*11   Lit. *of old, of Moses*
*c*14   So LXX; MT reads *gave them rest*

Relent,*d* for the sake of thy servants,
   the tribes that are thine inheritance.
¹⁸ But a little while
   had thy people possessed the holy place
   when our enemies trod down thy sanctuary.
¹⁹ We have become as those
   whom thou hast never ruled
   and who have not been known by thy name.

64

O that thou wouldst
   rend the heavens and descend,
   the mountains melting at thy presence—
² as when fire is lit for boiling water,
   which bubbles over from the heat—
to make thyself known to thine adversaries,
   the nations trembling at thy presence—
³ as when thou didst perform awesome things
   unexpected by us:
thy descent *of old*,
   when the mountains quaked before thee!
⁴ Never has it been heard
   or perceived by the ear,
nor has any eye seen a God besides thee,
   who acts thus
on behalf of those who wait for him.

⁵ But thou woundest those of us
   who joyfully perform righteousness,
and who remember thee by *following* thy ways
   *a*that in them we might be ever saved.*a*
Alas, thou wast roused to anger
   when we sinned,
⁶ and now we have altogether become
   as those defiled,
the sum of our righteousness
   as a menstruous rag.

*d*17   Or, *Return*
*a*5   Phrase transposed; in text follows *sinned*

We are decaying like leaves, all of us;
  our sins, like a wind, sweep us away.
⁷ Yet none calls upon thy name
  or rouses himself to take hold of thee;
for thou hast hidden thy face from us
  and enfeebled*b* us at the hand of our iniquities.

⁸ Nevertheless, thou art our Father, O Lord;
  we are the clay and thou art the potter,
and we are all alike
  the work of thy hands.*c*
⁹ Be not exceedingly angry, O Lord;
  remember not iniquity forever.
  See, consider that we are all thy people!
¹⁰ Thy holy cities have become a wilderness;
  Zion is a desert, Jerusalem a desolation.
¹¹ Our glorious holy temple
  where our fathers praised thee
has been burned with fire,
  and all places dear to us lie in ruins.
¹² At all this, O Lord,
  wilt thou restrain thyself,
in silence letting us suffer so exceedingly?

65

I was available to those
  who did not inquire of me;*a*
I was accessible to those
  who did not seek me.
I said, Here am I; I am here,
  to a nation that did not invoke my name.
² I held out my hands all the day
  to a defiant people,
who walk in ways that are not good,
  following their own imagination—

*b*7 Lit. *melted*
*c*8 So 1QIsaᵃ; LXX; cf. 60.21, etc. MT reads *hand*
*a*1 So 1QIsaᵃ; LXX; pronoun lacking in MT

³a people who constantly provoke me
  to my face,
 sacrificing in parks,
  making smoke upon bricks,
⁴who sit in sepulchres,
  spend nights in hideouts,
 who eat swine's flesh,
  their bowls full of polluted broth,
⁵who think, Keep your distance,
  don't come near me; I am holier than you!
 Such are a smoke to my nostrils,
  a fire smouldering all day long.
⁶See, it is written before me
  that I will not be still
 till I have paid back*ᵇ* into their bosom
   ⁷their*ᶜ* own iniquities and their*ᶜ* fathers' alike,
   says the Lord.
 To those who kindle sacrifice in the mountains,
  who affront me on the hills,
 I will measure out in their laps
  the payment that has accrued.

⁸Thus says the Lord:
  As when there is juice in a cluster of grapes
 and someone says, Don't destroy it,
  it is still good,
 so I will do on behalf of my servants
  by not destroying everything:
⁹I will extract offspring out of Jacob,
  and out of Judah heirs of my mountains;
 my chosen ones shall inherit them,
  my servants shall dwell there.
¹⁰Sharon shall become pasture for flocks,
  and the Valley of Achor a resting place
 for the herds of my people
  who seek me.

b6   Text adds *and paid back*, a probable duplication
c7   So LXX; MT reads *your*

11 As for you who forsake the Lord
and forget my holy mountain,
who spread tables for Luck
and pour mixed wines for Fortune,
12 I will destine you to the sword;
all of you shall succumb to the slaughter.
For when I called, you did not respond;
when I spoke, you would not give heed.
You did what was evil in my eyes;
you chose to do what was not my will.

13 Therefore thus says my Lord the Lord:
My servants shall eat indeed,
while you shall hunger;
my servants shall drink indeed,
while you shall thirst;
my servants shall rejoice indeed,
while you shall be dismayed.
14 My servants shall shout indeed,
for gladness of heart,
while you shall cry out with heartbreak,
howling from brokenness of spirit.
15 Your name shall be left
to serve my chosen ones as a curse
when my Lord the Lord slays you.
But his servants
he will call by a different name.
16 Those of them who invoke blessings
on themselves in the earth
shall do so by the true God,
and those of them who swear oaths in the earth
shall do so by the God of truth.
The troubles of the past shall be forgotten
and hidden from my eyes.

17 See, I create new heavens and a new earth;
former events shall not be remembered
or recalled to mind.

¹⁸ Rejoice, then, and be glad forever
    in what I create.
See, I create Jerusalem to be a delight
    and its people a joy.

¹⁹ I will delight in Jerusalem,
    rejoice in my people;
no more shall be heard there
    the sound of weeping
    or the cry of distress.
²⁰ No more shall there be
    infants alive but a few days,
    or the aged who do not live out their years;
those who die young
    shall be a hundred years old,
and those who fail to reach a hundred
    shall be accursed.
²¹ When men build houses,
    they will dwell in them;
when they plant vineyards,
    they will eat their fruit.
²² They shall not build so that others may dwell,
    or plant so that others may eat.
The lifetime of my people
    shall be as the lifetime of a tree;
my chosen ones shall outlast
    the work of their hands.
²³ They shall not exert themselves in vain,
    or bear children doomed for calamity.
For they are of the lineage of those
    blessed by the Lord,
    and their posterity with them.
²⁴ Before they call
    I will reply;
while they are speaking
    I will respond.

²⁵ The wolf and the lamb will graze alike,
and the lion will eat straw like the ox;
as for the serpent, dust shall be its food:
there shall be no harm or injury done
throughout my holy mountain,
says the Lord.

66 Thus says the Lord:
The heavens are my throne
and the earth is my footstool.
What house would you build me?
What would serve me as a place of residence?
² These are all things my hand has made,
and thus all came into existence,
says the Lord.
And yet I have regard for those
who are of a humble and contrite spirit
and who are vigilant for my word.

³ But whoever slaughters an ox
is as one who kills a man,
and whoever sacrifices a lamb,
as one who breaks a dog's neck;
whoever presents a grain offering
is as one who offers swine's blood,
and whoever burns incense,
as one who venerates idols.
Just as they have preferred to go their own ways,
their souls delighting in their abominations,
⁴ so will I prescribe intrigues for them
and bring upon them the thing they dread.
For when I called, no one responded;
when I spoke, none gave heed.
They did what was evil in my eyes;
they chose to do what was not my will.

⁵ Hear the word of the Lord,
you who are vigilant for his word:

Your brethren who abhor you,
    and exclude you because of my name, say,
Let the Lord manifest his glory,^a
    that we may see cause for your joy!
But it is they who shall suffer shame.
⁶ Hark, a tumult from the city,
    a noise from the temple!
It is the voice of the Lord
    paying his enemies what is due them.

⁷ Before she is in labor,
    she gives birth;
before her ordeal overtakes her,
    she delivers a son!
⁸ Who has heard the like,
    or who has seen such things?
Can the earth labor but a day
    and a nation be born at once?
For as soon as she was in labor,
    Zion gave birth to her children.
⁹ Shall I bring to a crisis and not bring on birth?
    says the Lord.
When it is I who cause the birth,
    shall I hinder it? says your God.
¹⁰ Rejoice with Jerusalem and be glad for her,
    all who love her;
join in her celebration,
    all who mourn for her.
¹¹ From now on nurse contentedly
    at her consoling breasts;
draw at your pleasure
    from the abundance of her bosom.^b

¹² For thus says the Lord:
    See, I will extend peace to her
    like a river,

[a]5   Or, *presence*
[b]11   Or, *glory*

the bounty*b* of the nations
like a stream in flood.
Then shall you nurse
and be carried upon the hip
and dandled on the knees.
¹³ As one who is comforted by his mother
I will comfort you;
for Jerusalem you shall be comforted.

¹⁴ Your heart shall rejoice to see it,
your limbs flourish like sprouting grass,
when the hand of the Lord
shall be manifest among his servants
and his rage among his enemies.
¹⁵ See, the Lord comes with fire,
his chariots like a whirlwind,
to retaliate in furious anger,
to rebuke with conflagrations of fire.
¹⁶ For with fire and with his sword shall the Lord
execute judgment upon all flesh,
and those slain by the Lord shall be many.

¹⁷ As for the cultists who absolve themselves in the parks, the devotees of those who are the center *of attraction*, who eat the flesh of swine and prawn and rodents—they with [their practices and ideas]*c* shall be made an end of, says the Lord.
¹⁸ For I will come*d* to gather all nations and tongues, that they may approach and behold my glory.*e*
¹⁹ And I will set a mark upon them, sending those of them who survive to the nations that had not heard the news concerning me, nor seen my glory*e*—to Tarshish, Pul and Lud (the archers), to Tubal and Javan, and to the distant isles. And they shall declare my glory*e* among the nations,

*b*12   Or, *glory*
*c*17   Terms brought up from verse 18, where they follow *For I*
*d*18   Heb. *bāʾâ, come* (fem. sing.) emended to *bāʾ*
*e*18, *e*19   Or, *presence*

²⁰ and shall bring back all your brethren from throughout the nations to Jerusalem my holy mountain, says the Lord, as offerings to the Lord—on horses, in chariots and wagons, and on mules and dromedaries—just as the Israelites brought offerings in pure vessels to the house of the Lord. ²¹ Of them likewise I will accept men to be priests and Levites, says the Lord.

²² And as the new heavens and the new earth which I make shall endure before me, says the Lord, so shall your offspring and name endure. ²³ And New Moon after New Moon, Sabbath after Sabbath, all flesh shall come to worship before me, says the Lord. ²⁴ And they shall go out and look upon the corpses of the people who transgressed against me, whose worms do not die and whose fire shall not be extinguished. They shall be a horror to all flesh.

Selected Reference Works

Alcalay, Reuben. *The Complete English-Hebrew, Hebrew-English Dictionary.* Jerusalem: Massada, 1970.

Biblia Hebraica, ed. Rudolf Kittel. Stuttgart: Württembergische Bibelanstalt, 1973.

Brown, Francis, S. R. Driver, and Charles A. Briggs. *A Hebrew and English Lexicon of the Old Testament.* Oxford: Clarendon, 1974.

Burrows, Millar. *The Dead Sea Scrolls of St. Mark's Monastery.* Vol. 1. New Haven: American Schools of Oriental Research, 1950.

Even-Shoshan, Avraham. *Hamilon Hehadash.* 3 vols. Jerusalem: Sivan, 1975.

Guillaume, Alfred. 'Some Readings in the Dead Sea Scroll of Isaiah.' *JBL* (1957), 40-43.

Hulst, A. R. *Old Testament Translation Problems.* Leiden: Brill, 1960.

James, Forrest D. 'A Critical Examination of the Text of Isaiah.' Ph.D. dissertation, Boston University, 1959.

Mandelkern, Solomon. *Veteris Testamenti Concordantiae.* Tel Aviv: Schocken, 1974.

Rosenbloom, Joseph R. *The Dead Sea Isaiah Scroll: A Literary Analysis.* Grand Rapids: Eerdmans, 1970.

The Interpreter's Bible. Vol. 5. Nashville: Abingdon, 1956.

The Septuagint Version. Grand Rapids: Zondervan, 1970.

Young, Robert. *Analytical Concordance to the Bible.* New York: Funk and Wagnall's, 1973.

An Apocalyptic Key

Abbreviations

ANET	J. B. Pritchard (ed.), *Ancient Near Eastern Texts*
BA	*Biblical Archaeologist*
Bib	*Biblica*
CBQ	*Catholic Biblical Quarterly*
Enc	*Encounter*
HUCA	*Hebrew Union College Annual*
IB	*Interpreter's Bible*
Int	*Interpretation*
JAOS	*Journal of the American Oriental Society*
JBL	*Journal of Biblical Literature*
VT	*Vetus Testamentum*
ZAW	*Zeitschrift für die alttestamentliche Wissenschaft*

An Apocalyptic Key

a. Isaianic Scholarship and its Effects. The history of modern scholarship on the Book of Isaiah need not be detailed here. The briefest survey would show that the tendency among scholars to fragment the text has resulted in a serious oversight: failure to consider basic literary structures and patterns that tie together all parts of the book. The very nature of the two chief methods of biblical criticism, the traditio-historical and form-critical approaches, seems to discount a view of the Book of Isaiah as a whole. The book's three distinct historical settings, and its divided content of prophetic oracles and written discourses, are regarded as grounds for the belief that the book has diverse origins: that its sections represent separate entities. Although these two approaches to Isaianic scholarship have brought many valuable things to light, much has nevertheless been overlooked because of their limitations. Only recently have several prominent scholars of the traditio-historical and form-critical schools of biblical criticism taken seriously the idea of the Book of Isaiah as a literary unity—not as a result of their methods, but as an intuitive reach for what lies beyond their scope. However, in view of evidence of the book's literary unity, a complete rethinking is required to assure this prophetic text not remain, in effect, a sealed book. Without consideration of its literary structure and typology, scholarly attempts at its interpretation must fall short of the mark. On the other hand, when these aspects are considered, the Book of Isaiah unfolds as a coherent and truly prophetic masterpiece of Hebrew literature.

b. A Structural Synthesis. The literary framework of the Book of Isaiah consists of four kinds of composites or syntheses; although these make the book complex, an understanding of them is the key to its interpretation. The first of these, a Structural Synthesis, is composed of five

171

literary structures, every one spanning the length of the book, in addition to a number of smaller, localized patterns.[1] The most complex is the Bifid structure, consisting partly of the division of the Book of Isaiah into two halves, each of which divides into seven categories of parallel subject matter,[2] as follows:

Part I (Chapters 1-33)	Part II (Chapters 34-66)
a b c d e f g	a b c d e f g

This mechanical division serves to convey an underlying message, for besides sharing common subject matter, each category of the first block progresses in thought to its counterpart in the second block. In other words, an idea or concept that appears in Part I, *a* reappears in Part II, *a* but in a more developed form. In addition to this, each concept thus developed is cumulative: a concept developed in one set of parallel categories is presupposed in the next, climaxing in the seventh, where Isaianic thought occurs fully developed. Needless to say, the underlying message of this structure consists of these cumulative concepts, not of the categories themselves. Each of the three syntheses discussed later—the Synthesis of Events, Entity Synthesis and Covenant Synthesis—is implicit to this development within the Bifid structure. As in every broad structure of the Book of Isaiah, the most obvious phenomenon is the subordination of historical material to a higher purpose: the creation of a new stage of events depicting the last days. More simply stated, this means that when viewed as part of a literary structure, entities and events which occur in history in the Book of Isaiah assume new roles as patterns or types for those in the future. The anonymous 'king of Assyria,' for example, may refer to at least one king who can be historically identified in the ancient Near East. Within the Bifid structure, however, he serves as the model or type for an arch-Tyrant of the last days who is overthrown by an ideal Davidic king (see II, **b. An Entity Synthesis**). Likewise, the Assyrian conquest of the ancient world, as depicted by Isaiah, serves as the precedent or type for a conquest of the

---

[1]Explications of these structural syntheses are condensations of parts of the writer's Ph.D. dissertation, *A Holistic Structure of the Book of Isaiah,* 1981, and parts of a forthcoming book entitled *The Structure and Typology of the Book of Isaiah.*

[2]Viz., Ruin and Renascence, chs. 1-5; 34-35; Biographical Material, chs. 6-8; 36-40; Agents of Divine Deliverance and Judgment, chs. 9-12; 41-46; Oracles Against Foreign Powers, chs. 13-23; 47; Suffering and Salvation, chs. 24-27; 48-54; Sermons on Loyalty and Disloyalty, chs. 28-31; 55-59; Dispossession of the Wicked, Inheritance by the Righteous, chs. 32-33; 60-66.

world in the last days by a power that fits remarkably well the mold of the former (see II, **a. A Synthesis of Events**). It is the Bifid structure that lays a foundation for this higher (eschatological) function of Isaianic prophecies, as expressed in the other three syntheses.

Superimposed upon the complex Bifid structure in the Book of Isaiah are four structures which appear to be influenced by patterns existing in ancient Near Eastern literatures before the lifetime of Isaiah. One consists of the threefold narrative plot: Trouble at Home, Exile Abroad, and Happy Homecoming. It occurs as early as the Twelfth Dynasty in Egypt in such stories as *Sinuhe, The Shipwrecked Sailor, The Two Brothers, The Foredoomed Prince*, and *The Blinding of Truth by Error*.[3] In the Egyptian narrative, exemplified by the story of Sinuhe, the hero, who is part of an established community, is forced to flee into the world at large, where his interaction with people and events causes him to awaken to his true identity. At that point he is welcomed back, escorted home, and received with much fanfare, to be appointed to high office and standing in his native community. The threefold theme, which today forms the basis of many fairy tales, is also the story of Israel's patriarch Jacob in his flight from Esau (see Gen. 27.41-45; 29.1) and his return home at divine bidding (Gen. 31.13-18; 32.1; 35.9-12). In the Book of Isaiah it coincides with the loss and recovery of Paradise, and is reflected in the book's three distinctive settings for Israel: before the Exile (Chapters 1-39), during the Exile (Chapters 40-54), and after the Exile (Chapters 55-66). These settings further correspond to three distinctive characterizations of Israel, namely, as a national entity (Chapters 1-39), a universal entity (Chapters 40-54), and an entity composed of certain (repentant) individuals (Chapters 55-66). As may be expected, this progress from nationalism to universalism to individualism, characterizing Israel, is cumulative. In the last days, the Israel that returns home at divine bidding is a nation of awakened individuals (see 55.1-6) who had merged and become identified with the world at large (see 41.8-9; 46.3-8). Those who return from the four directions are those who respond to a universal call to repent (see 44.22; 45.22). Upon being proven, they participate in a dramatic event in which a new nation is born (see 66.4-8).

Far from providing grounds for viewing separately the three different settings of the Book of Isaiah, the above threefold structure thus demands a total view of the text. As in all major literary structures of the

---

[3] See Adolf Erman, *The Ancient Egyptians,* New York: Harper and Row, 1966; Alan H. Gardiner, *Hieratic Papyri, Third Series*, London: British Museum, 1935; John A. Wilson, in J. B. Pritchard, ed., *Ancient Near Eastern Texts*, Princeton: Princeton University, 1969 (hereafter designated as *ANET*).

Book of Isaiah, the author follows in detail a carefully planned literary scheme that conveys an underlying message: Israel, because of its rebellion against its covenant Lord, finds itself in trouble in its homeland (see 1.21-24). Divine reprisals force it abroad into the world for a protracted stay (see 5.13; 6.11). There it intermingles with peoples and assimilates their lifestyle and idolatry (see 42.17-20; 48.1-8). Gaining awareness, certain individuals reject the practices of the world, are refined by persecution, and answer a prophetic call to gather home (see 51.7-11; 55.4-12). Those who return are exalted as kings and priests (see 61.3, 6; 62.1-3), while those who remain incur the calamities which immediately follow (see 57.1-13). What distinguishes this and every major literary structure of the Book of Isaiah is that the end is foreseen from the beginning (see I, c). One cannot therefore treat separately the parts from the whole, as scholars have done, or the message is lost from view.

A third literary structure of the Book of Isaiah consists of the fourfold succession of themes: Apostasy (Chapters 1-9), Judgment (Chapters 10-34), Restoration (Chapters 35-59), and Salvation (Chapters 60-66). Each of these four themes also occurs in localized instances throughout the book; together they account for much of its content. Such localized instances, however, should not be confused with the broad sequence of the four themes that governs the material as a whole. Localized instances of the themes, as in the first six chapters of the book, actually furnish the key to this sequence, if one allows for some variations. Although there is a general emphasis in these chapters upon the idea of Israel's Apostasy, the four themes of Apostasy, Judgment, Restoration, and Salvation occur repeatedly in order, accounting for the entire content of Chapters 1-6.[4]

Each of the four sections of the Book of Isaiah commences with the formal introduction of the entity who dominates in the section. In the section whose general theme is Apostasy, it is Israel itself, arraigned in a lawsuit (see 1.2, 10). Israel has revolted from its covenant Lord, has become utterly insensible, perverse and sick, and has degenerated to the condition of a slave (see 1.3-6). Israel, though granted a period of probation in which to mend its ways (see 1.19-20), fails to do so (see 9.13-17). Formally presented at the beginning of the next section on Judgment is

---

[4] Viz., A. 1.2-6; J. 1.7-8; R. 1.10; S. 1.9; A. 1.11-14; J. 1.15; R. 1.16-18; S. 1.19; A. 1.20-23; J. 1.24; R. 1.25-26; S. 1.27; A. 1.28-29; J. 1.30-31; R. 2.2-3; S. 2.4-5; A. 2.6-9; J. 2.10-17; R. 2.18; J. 2.19-21; A. 2.22; J. 3.1-4; A. 3.5-9; S. 3.10; J. 3.11-14; A. 3.15-16; J. 3.17-4.1; R. 4.2; S. 4.3; J. 4.4; R. 4.5-5.3; A. 5.4; J. 5.5-6; A. 5.7-8; J. 5.9-10; A. 5.11-12; J. 5.13-14; A. 5.15; J. 5.16a; R. 5.16b; S. 5.17; A. 5.18-23; J. 5.24-30; R. 6.1-2; S. 6.3; A. 6.4-5; J. 6.6; R. 6.7a; S. 6.7b-8; A. 6.9-10; J. 6.11-13b; R. S. 6.13c.

the king of Assyria (see 10.5). There comes a day of reckoning when the Lord's anger is kindled against his people, and he selects as his *rod* of punishment the Assyrian Tyrant (see 10.3-6). This destroyer by fire and by war gains possession of the whole world by force (see 10.7-14), with the exception of a small remnant loyal to the Lord (see 10.20-22; 33.1-22). Restoration coincides with the prophetic announcement of the coming of Israel's God (see 35.4). At his coming, the earth itself is to be regenerated and restored to its paradisaical glory, and Israel ransomed and healed (see 35.1-10). The Assyrian horde is to be exterminated in a classic instance of divine intervention, as it seeks to deal the death blow to Israel by advancing against its loyal remnant (see 37.32-36). The covenantal nature of Israel's redemption throughout the earth is detailed (see 44.21-26; 49.8-26), including the part played in this redemption by an ideal Davidic ruler as well as by the Lord himself (see below). The theme of Salvation dominates from the time of the Lord's coming in power and glory to establish his rule on earth (see 59.19-60.3). The exaltation of his people and destruction of his enemies are now consummated, and Israel and the earth are created anew (see 65.12-25; 66.6-22).

The fourfold structure of Apostasy, Judgment, Restoration, and Salvation again appears to be based on ancient Near Eastern literary patterns in existence before the time of Isaiah. It corresponds to the cycle of themes, Threat, War, Victory, and Feast, of Canaanite mythology, which occurs as a further key in Chapters 24-27 and elsewhere.[5] In the Ugaritic myth of Baal and Anat, the storm god Baal, a contender for the throne, is threatened by his rival Yamm/Nahar.[6] After a fierce rivalry and battle, the latter is overpowered,[7] and fertility restored to the earth. Baal's victory is celebrated with a sumptuous feast in the presence of his daughters. A variation of this cycle repeats itself in Baal's victory over Mot (Death), god of the underworld. In the Book of Isaiah, however, the themes of Threat, War, Victory, and Feast are transformed into the Hebrew prophetic forms of Apostasy, Judgment, Restoration, and Salvation—to convey the message that Israel's history does not end with its Apostasy and Judgment, but continues with its Restoration and Salvation according to a predetermined plan. Within this scheme of

[5] See William R. Millar, *Isaiah 24-27 and the Origin of Apocalyptic*, Missoula: Scholars Press, 1976. Millar's study unfortunately flounders amid historical presuppositions and fails to note the incidence of mythical patterns throughout the Book of Isaiah, as well as their transformation into Hebrew prophetic forms.

[6] I.e., Sea/River; see these powers of chaos as pseudonyms of the king of Assyria, 5.30; 8.7-8; 11.15, etc.

[7] See the Lord as storm god, in battle with Assyria, 30.30, 31.

175

Israel's Restoration and Salvation all the earth and its inhabitants may participate, for outside of this there is only Apostasy and Judgment; common to all major literary structures of the Book of Isaiah is the concept that ultimately no Salvation or plan of Salvation exists outside of Israel. In the light of the extensive localized use of the fourfold pattern in the Book of Isaiah, it would thus be partial to view the themes of Apostasy and Judgment of the broad structure separate from those of Restoration and Salvation—just as it would be partial to do the reverse. Even more inadequate than such a partial view of the book would be the isolation of one theme from the others. Within Israel's covenant relationship with its God, Judgment follows naturally upon Apostasy as a consequence of divine justice, and Restoration upon Judgment by virtue of the Lord's twin attribute of mercy, or righteousness; Salvation is the end result for those who endure loyal to Israel's God. A total view of this fourfold pattern is thus essential if its message is to be transmitted intact.

A fourth broad structure consists of a division of the Book of Isaiah according to the curses and blessings pattern of ancient Near Eastern treaties. The literary form of the Sinai covenant has been seen by scholars to resemble that of Hittite and Assyrian suzerain-vassal treaties,[8] in which the Lord assumes the role of suzerain or Great King and Israel that of his vassal or tenant king. So too in the Book of Isaiah, an emphasis upon Covenantal Malediction (Chapters 1-39) derives from the legal prosecution of the vassal Israel by its suzerain Lord. Israel's breaking of the covenant is expressed in moralistic terms: the Lord's *sons* (an ancient Near Eastern synonym for *vassals*) have *rebelled* (1.2) and are *wayward* (1.5). Heaven and Earth, witnesses of the Sinai covenant (Deut. 30.19), are called upon to testify of Israel's rebellion (1.2); and covenant curses (Malediction) take effect as punishment (1.5-9). With some localized exceptions, the general tone of Covenantal Malediction is maintained throughout Chapters 1-39. In later chapters of this section, Covenantal Malediction extends to the nations, for in Isaianic thought, all peoples of the earth, except those who form the new Israel at his coming, are ultimately seen to be in rebellion against Israel's God. An emphasis on Covenantal Benediction (Chapters 40-66) commences

[8] See George E. Mendenhall, 'Covenant Forms in Israelite Tradition,' *BA*, 17.3 (1954), pp. 50-76; F. C. Fensham, 'Malediction and Benediction in Ancient Near Eastern Vassal-Treaties and the Old Testament,' *ZAW*, 74 (1962), pp. 1-8; David Noel Freedman, 'Divine Commitment and Human Obligation,' *Int*, 18 (1964), pp. 410-31; Moshe Weinfeld, 'Traces of Assyrian Treaty Formulary in Deuteronomy,' *Bib*, 46 (1965), pp. 417-27; W. Eichrodt, 'Covenant and Law,' *Int*, 20 (1966), pp. 302-21.

with the formal pronouncement by Israel's covenant Lord that a national debt has been paid (40.1, 2). Israel, which has *served its term*, paid *double for all its sins* (40.2), is told to prepare for the return of its absentee Lord (40.5, 9, 10). Covenantal Benediction takes the form not merely of blessings, but of curse reversals, a phenomenon not known outside of Israel and therefore representing a transformation of ancient Near Eastern treaty patterns.

Coinciding with Covenantal Malediction and Benediction in the Book of Isaiah are the dominant themes of Chaos (Chapters 1-39) and Creation (Chapters 40-66). Exceptions throughout the book take the form of localized patterns of Chaos and Creation, the two themes alternating most prominently in Chapters 1-12 and 40-46.[9] A theological message suggested by this pattern is that there cannot be Creation without a preceding Chaos, a concept that accords with the Genesis account of the Creation (see Gen. 1.2) and with ancient Near Eastern mythologies,[10] of which it is a transformation. The emphasis by scholars upon Creation and Israel's redemption in the second section of the Book of Isaiah[11] is thus one-sided. There exists in the first section a corresponding emphasis on Chaos and on Israel's transgression. The interrelationship in the Book of Isaiah between Chaos and Creation, both localized and on a broad scale, similarly characterizes Covenantal Malediction and Benediction: there can evidently be no curse reversals (Covenantal Benediction) without prior curses (Covenantal Malediction). However, just as Chaos and Creation are linked to Israel's transgression and redemption, so are Covenantal Malediction and Benediction: covenant curses (Malediction) take place when Israel transgresses, a situation characterized by Chaos; curse reversals (Benediction) take place at Israel's

---

[9] Viz., Ch. 1.25; C. 1.26; Ch. 1.31; C. 2.2-5; Ch. 3.25-26; C. 4.2; Ch. 4.4; C. 4.5; Ch. 5.24, 25, 30; C. 6.1-4; Ch. 9.1; C. 9.2, 6-7; Ch. 10.33-34; C. 11.1-2; Ch. 40.7-8a; C. 40.8b, 12-13; Ch. 40.15-17, 20; C. 40.21-22; Ch. 40.23-24; C. 40.26, 28-29; Ch. 40.30; C. 40.31; Ch. 41.2, 15-16; C. 41.17-20; Ch. 41.25, 29; C. 42.1-6; Ch. 42.15; C. 42.16; Ch. 42.17, 22, 24-25; C. 43.1; Ch. 43.14; C. 43.15; Ch. 43.16-17; C. 43.19-21; Ch. 43.22; C. 44.1-4; Ch. 44.9, 11-12, 18, 20; C. 44.21; Ch. 44.22; C. 44.24; Ch. 44.25; C. 44.26; Ch. 44.27; C. 44.28; Ch. 45.1-2; C. 45.3-8; Ch. 45.9; C. 45.11-13; Ch. 45.16; C. 45.17-18; Ch. 46.1-2; C. 46.10-11.

[10] See the 'Creation Epic,' *ANET*, pp. 60-72; Henri Frankfort, *Kingship and the Gods*, Chicago: University of Chicago, 1948, p. 150; Bernhard W. Anderson, *Creation Versus Chaos*, New York: Association Press, 1967, pp. 11-42.

[11] See Carroll Stuhlmueller, 'The Theology of Creation in Second Isaiah,' *CBQ*, 21 (1959), pp. 429-67; *Creative Redemption in Deutero-Isaiah*, Rome: Pontifical Biblical Institute, 1970.

redemption, a situation characterized by Creation. An underlying message of this literary structure, therefore, is that there can be no redemption for Israel without Israel's transgression. Such a conclusion may seem simplistic until one realizes that it concerns all the earth; what began with Israel's transgression ends with the redemption of all who repent and the earth's return to its paradisaical glory—as part of a predetermined plan. Both politically and theologically the nations of the earth are identified with Israel: politically because they were once part of its empire (see 1 Kings 4.21, 24; 8.65),[12] and because Israel has since mingled and become identified with the nations (see Deut. 28.64)[13]; theologically because covenant curses in the Book of Isaiah extend as much to the nations as they do to Israel (see esp. 24.5), and because all are accepted into the covenant who prove loyal to Israel's God (see 56.1-8; 66.18-21). The above literary structure of Covenantal Malediction and Covenantal Benediction is thus another that bridges the gap between Israel's ancient history and the last days, the time of the return of Israel's covenant Lord.

Two additional structures of the Book of Isaiah detail the nature of Israel's redemption, and thus are closely linked to the preceding two. The first of these, a broad structure, deals with a temporal deliverance from mortal danger; the second, a major internal structure, deals with spiritual salvation from sin. Both temporal deliverance and spiritual salvation comprise Israel's redemption, which thus has two aspects. The first consists of the pattern: Destruction of the Wicked (Chapters 1-34), Deliverance of the Righteous (Chapters 40-66), through divine intervention by virtue of a Loyal Davidic King (Chapters 35-39). This pattern, called Isaianic Zion Ideology, and based on the idea of divine protection deriving from the Davidic covenant, occurs in localized instances throughout the Book of Isaiah.[14] In these localized instances, the Davidic ruler may appear under one of several pseudonyms, namely, the

---

[12] See G. Ernest Wright, 'The Nations in Hebrew Prophecy,' *Enc*, 26 (1965), pp. 225-37; John Mauchline, 'Implicit Signs of a Persistent Belief in the Davidic Empire,' *VT*, 20 (1970), pp. 287-303.

[13] See D. E. Hollenberg, 'Nationalism and "The Nation" in Isaiah XL-LV,' *VT*, 19 (1969), pp. 23-36; and II, **b. An Entity Synthesis**.

[14] Viz., 1.24-28; 1.31-2.4; 4.2-6; 8.8-18; 10.24-11.1; 14.29-32; 16.1, 4, 5; 17.12-18.4, 7; 24: 21-23; 25.8-12; 26.1-5; 28.15-18; 29.1, 7, 8; 30.17-20, 27-33; 31.4-32.1; 33.3-6; 33.12-17; 33.20-34.2; 34.5-8, 17; 37.32-36; 46.11-47.1; 49.13-26; 51.3-8; 51.9-11; 51.16-23; 52.7-12; 59.16-20; 62.1-3; 62.10-63.6; 66.6-8.

Lord's *hand*, his *ensign*, *righteousness*, etc.; but all three elements of the pattern are present.

The Davidic covenant, which is modeled upon the ancient Near Eastern Covenant of Grant,[15] contains a protection clause to the effect that the suzerain (the Lord) undertakes to protect the people of the vassal, providing the vassal (the Davidic king) is loyal to the suzerain (see Psa. 89.19-37; 1 Kings 6.12-13; 9.2-7). In accordance with suzerain-vassal agreements in general, there was also a protection clause in the Sinai covenant, and during the Conquest of Canaan, when all Israel was loyal to the Lord, it received divine protection. If one man transgressed, however, divine protection was withheld and all Israel suffered reverses (see Josh. 7.1-26). After the Conquest, when Israel's loyalty to its covenant Lord lapsed, divine protection also lapsed, and by the time of Samuel and Saul, Israel's enemies threatened the very life of the nation. Israel then sought another means of national protection, a king who would rally all the tribes to battle (see 1 Sam. 8.20; 2 Sam. 5.2). The Davidic covenant, vested in a king loyal to the Lord, was a divine response to this need for national protection. From then on, according to the terms of the Lord's separate agreement with David and his ruling descendants, national protection depended only on the king's loyalty to the Lord. Those loyal to the king received divine protection by proxy so long as the king (the vassal) was loyal to the Lord (the suzerain). Appended to the Davidic covenant was thus the idea of Zion as a safe place, because in Zion the Lord 'put his name,' an expression denoting that he was present there (see Deut. 12.5-14; Isa. 18.7; Psa. 132.11-18).

In the Book of Isaiah, the Lord's presence among and divine protection for Israel are notably absent in the section Destruction of the Wicked (Chapters 1-34). Israel is classed among enemies who are destroyed, though provision is made for the survival of a remnant (see 1.24-28; 6.13; 10.20-23, etc.). On the other hand, in the section Deliverance of the Righteous (Chapters 40-66), the Lord's presence among Israel is a key idea (see esp. 40.5, 9-10; 52.6-10; 62.11), and the theme of Israel's deliverance pervades the section (see 41.8-20; 43.1-8; 44.1-6, etc.). In the intermediate section A Loyal Davidic King (Chapters 35-39), divine protection is linked to the role of the model king, Hezekiah. In a classic instance of Isaianic Zion Idealogy, a remnant of Israel, besieged in Zion, receives divine protection against the Assyrian threat (see 37.32-36) 'for my [the Lord's] own sake and for the sake of my servant David' (verse 35). The latter expression signifies that the terms of the Davidic covenant

---

[15] See Moshe Weinfeld, 'The Covenant of Grant in the Old Testament and in the Ancient Near East,' *JAOS*, 90 (1970), pp. 184-203; 'Berith,' in Botterweck and Ringgren, *Theological Dictionary of the Old Testament*, Vol. 2, Grand Rapids: Eerdmans, 1977.

are being met by both parties to the covenant, a loyal vassal and a faithful suzerain. Such divine protection does not happen, however, without a severe test of both people and king. As a test, the Assyrian king plays the role of an alternate suzerain or Great King (36.4, 13), seeking to win the loyalties of the people and their king with sweet promises (36.16-17). Faced with either changing their loyalties or annihilation, the people remain loyal to King Hezekiah (36.21-22) and Hezekiah to the Lord (37.1-4, 14-20). The king's loyalty is then further tested under the duress of a mortal *illness* (an ancient Near Eastern synonym of *covenant love*), which he again passes, receiving the assurance of his own recovery and the deliverance of his people (38.1-6). These tests of loyalty passed, the Lord responds with the annihilation of the threatening Assyrian army (37.36), thus delivering the remnant of his people.

The historical role of King Hezekiah as a type of an ideal Davidic king occurs in the Book of Isaiah in contrast to the role of his father Ahaz. King Ahaz' loyalty to the Lord was similarly tested, though he failed the test (see 7.4-7). In sending tribute money to the king of Assyria and referring to himself as his *servant* and *son* (synonyms for *vassal*), Ahaz made the latter his suzerain (see 2 Kings 16.7-8). In accordance with ancient Near Eastern treaty procedure, the Lord's first response to Ahaz' disloyalty was to choose another *son*/vassal, namely Immanuel (7.14); his second response was to deny divine protection (7.17-20). The king's disloyalty to the Lord coincided with the people's disloyalty to the king in their rejection of the 'waters of Shiloah' (8.6), a symbol of Davidic rule.[16] For this apostasy, the king of Assyria, cast in the mythological role of a *River* in flood, was to sweep through the land of Immanuel (8.7-8) and reach 'the neck,' which is Zion. This was fulfilled in the case of King Hezekiah, as outlined above, for the name Immanuel (*God is with us*) above all signifies divine protection: when the Lord is present *with* the people, there is an assurance of protection (see Psa. 46.5-7); where he is not, there is no assurance of protection (see 8.17-22; 10.3-7; 28.14-19, etc.). Because the present literary structure subordinates these historical accounts, one must concede a new (eschatological) setting for the Book of Isaiah: Hezekiah foreshadows the role of an ideal Davidic king of the last days, the time of the Lord's return, and Ahaz the role of an apostate king, his contemporary (cf. Saul and David, 1 Sam. 15.26-16.3). Because of a vassal loyal to the suzerain, the Lord will be *with* those loyal to the king, delivering them

---

[16] See their source, Gihon, as a coronation site of Davidic monarchs, 1 Kings 1.38-39. The name of the substitute ruler proposed by Rezin and Pekah, the so-called 'son of Tabeal' (7.6), in treaty language translates 'non-covenantal vassal,' to denote a non-Davidic (puppet) king.

at his coming to Zion (see 35.4, 10). The underlying message of this threefold pattern in the Book of Isaiah, both localized and on a broad scale, thus excludes any provision for deliverance by divine intervention other than within the pattern: Destruction of the Wicked, Deliverance of the Righteous, by virtue of a Loyal Davidic King. Contrary to an assumption by scholars, moreover, the historical accounts in the section A Loyal Davidic King (Isa. 36-39) form an integral part of the Book of Isaiah when viewed within the above and other structures.

A final, internal structure of the Book of Isaiah concerns the second aspect of Israel's redemption, that of spiritual salvation from sin. This structure, whose main body I have named the Servant-Tyrant Parallelism, consists of a contrasting relationship between Zion and Babylon and between the king of Zion and the king of Babylon in the following passages:[17]

Isa. 47		*Isa.* 52	
1-4	Babylon dethroned, disrobed, in the dust—vengeance by Israel's God	1-3	Zion arises from the dust, clad in robes, enthroned—the Lord's redemption
Isa. 14			
1	Israel returned to its land—strangers cleave to them	4	Israel in exile—oppressed by foreigners
2	Israel's authority restored—rules over its oppressors	5	Israel's authority taken away—ruled by oppressors
*3	The Lord gives rest from sorrow and bondage in that day	*6	The Lord manifests his presence in that day
4	Bad tidings for Babylon—her king's reign of tyranny ends	7	Good tidings for Zion—her God's reign of peace begins
5	Babylon's wicked king is broken	8	The Lord returns to Zion as king
6	The Tyrant struck the nations in wrath	[10][18]	All nations see the Lord's saving arm

[17] Not contrasted, but complementary, are the third and seventh parallel verses of the main body, which thus contain a key message (see asterisks).

[18] Verse 10 of Chapter 52 appears out of sequence. The complementary nature of 52.9 and 14.7 is evident in their common element of jubilation (Heb. *pāṣḥû rinnâ*, 14.7; *piṣḥû rannēnû*, 52.9; Chapter 52 reads more coherently with the emendation.

*7 Jubilation—the whole earth
at rest and at peace

8 He who hewed down Israel
has gone out of her

9 The Tyrant in the company of
the dead; exiled to Sheol

10 The Tyrant is demeaned,
subjected to reproach

11 The ignominious Tyrant previously emjoyed eminence

12 He who subjected the nations
lamented in awe

13 The Tyrant *ascends* (Heb. root
ʿālâ) the heavens

14 The Tyrant aspires to be like
the Most High

15 The Tyrant's ignominy is final

16, 17ab The Tyrant causes havoc
and destruction

17c The Tyrant brings others into
permanent bondage

18 The kings of the nations die
with honor

19 The Tyrant is slain for his own
crimes

*9 Jubilation—Israel comforted,
redeemed

11 Those who bring back Israel's
descendants[19] go out of Babylon

12 Israel returns from exile in the
company of its God

13 The Servant is exalted, acquires
eminence

14 The eminent Servant previously
enjoyed ignominy

15 He who purges the nations
esteemed in awe

Isa. 53

1-2 The Servant[20] *grows up* (Heb.
root ʿālâ) out of the earth

3 The Servant submits to being
the lowest of men

4, 5ab The Servant's ignominy is
redemptive

5cd The Servant causes peace and
healing

6 The Servant atones for the sins
of others

7 The Servant goes like a lamb
to the slaughter

8 The Servant is slain for the
crimes of his people

---

[19] Lit. *vessels*, but see **22.24** for this symbolism.

[20] Although in 53.1-10 the term *Servant* is employed in the parallelism, it is justified only by analogy with the term used in 52.13; 53.11 (see the discussion below).

20ab	The Tyrant is unburied because he did violence	9	The Servant is buried because he did no violence
20c, 21	The Tyrant's offspring is slaughtered, to rise no more	10	The Servant sees his offspring perpetuated
22	Babylon's survivors cut off	11	Zion's Servant vindicates many
23	Babylon an inheritance for birds	12	Zion an inheritance for the Servant and those he redeems

Although this structure contains many analogical lessons as well as an underlying message, only a few points can be dealt with here. First, as with all broad structures of the Book of Isaiah, the Servant-Tyrant Parallelism lifts the entities of Babylon and the king of Babylon as well as Zion, the king of Zion and the suffering figure from a historical setting to a higher (eschatological) one. In other words, they do not deal with figures of history, at least history prior to that reflected in the Book of Isaiah, but with types for the future. A relationship between biblical entities such as the above simply did not exist, and one must therefore look beyond history for an interpretation.

Second, within the above structure, Zion's redemption is not consummated and Zion's king does not reign until Babylon is destroyed and its king deposed, where, as just noted, the terms *Zion* and *Babylon* refer to entities other than historical. The complementary third and seventh parallel verses further suggest that rest from bondage for Israel occurs in the presence of the Lord, and that universal peace ensues at the Lord's redemption of his people, both of which are consummated at his coming to reign.

Third, the structural contrast of both the king of Zion of Chapter 52 and the suffering figure of Chapter 53 with a single king of Babylon (throughout the greater part of the Servant-Tyrant Parallelism) teaches by analogy that the suffering figure *is* Israel's God, the king of Zion. The suffering figure's contrast with a suzerain (the king of Babylon) suggests that he himself is a suzerain; his coupling with the king of Zion as part of that contrast suggests that that suzerain is the king of Zion. The role of the suffering figure, given as that of atonement for the sins of his people (identified as *we/us*; see 53.4-6, 8, 10), is thus the role of Israel's God, who is identified elsewhere as the Redeemer of Israel from its sins (see 43.25; 44.22-23; 52.3, 9, etc.).

Another indication of the divinity of the suffering figure is that there exists no biblical type or precedent for one man's death to atone for the sins of others (see 53.5-8, 10).[21] Because the structure and content of the Book of Isaiah have for a literary framework the events of biblical history as types for the last days (see II, A Message of Content), the book's chief human characters have as their types the heroes and villains of biblical history. To this there is no exception. Since the concept of an atoning death by an individual for the sins of other individuals has no valid type in Israel's past, it must lie, typologically speaking, outside the sphere of purely human activity.

A fourth idea based on the analogical relationship of the two main figures of the Servant-Tyrant Parallelism is that what is said of one may, within a limited context, apply to the other. For example, the king of Babylon's aspiration to achieve an exalted divine status (14.13-14) may in reality describe the status of the suffering figure that contrasts with him. On the other hand, the ignominious suffering of the servant figure may in reality describe the fate of the king of Babylon. The existence of the Servant-Tyrant Parallelism in the Book of Isaiah may explain a statement in an ancient document attributed to Isaiah, that the Lord would descend to Sheol. A passage in the 'Ascension of Isaiah'[22] supposedly derives this idea by linking Isa. 52.13 to Chapters 13-14.[23] In the Servant-Tyrant Parallelism, the servant figure exalted in the realm of the living (52.13) is, in fact, contrasted with the king of Babylon, who is demoted to the realm of the dead (14.10). Because of the analogical relationship of these figures within the structure, however, what is said of the king of Babylon may, within a limited context, apply also to the

---

[21] The doctrine of spiritual atonement for sins nevertheless has a typological antecedent in animal sacrifice, in which an animal suffered the death due to a man who had sinned. Of course, the ritual itself did not spiritually cleanse the man, but symbolized the reality of purification by proxy.

[22] See the translation by J. Flemming and H. Duensing in Hennecke and Schneemelcher, *New Testament Apocrypha, Vol. II*, Philadelphia: Westminster, 1965.

[23] The passage in full states: 'The remainder of the words of the vision is recorded in the vision concerning Babylon [Isa. 13-14]. And the rest of the vision of the Lord, behold, it is recorded in parables in my words which are written in the book which I openly proclaimed. Moreover the descent of the Beloved into the realm of the dead is recorded in the section where the Lord says "Behold, my servant is prudent" [Isa. 52.13]' (Asc. Isa. 4.19-21).

servant figure. The idea of a god who descends to the underworld is well-known in ancient Near Eastern mythology.[24]

Also possessing parallels in mythology is the king of Babylon's ascent into the heavens,[25] whence he rules the world he has conquered by force (14.2-14). Because this is possible with today's technology, it does not lie beyond the reach of purely human activity. However, such a physical realization of an ascent to heaven is but a counterfeit of true (spiritual) exaltation (viz., that of 40.22; 66.1), which has no human type in biblical history and should therefore be viewed as lying beyond the reach of purely human attainment. On the other hand, what does have an important type within the above structure is the 'pouring out of one's soul unto death' and 'making intercession for transgressors' (53.12). The first was fulfilled by King Hezekiah during his illness (see 38.9-20), the second by Moses at Israel's idolatry (see Exod. 32.11-13). This suggests that a figure other than the suffering figure of 53.1-10 may be included as a subject of the passage, something also suggested by its divided dialogue. In 52.13-15 and 53.11-12, the Lord is the speaker and his *servant* (an ancient Near Eastern synonym for *vassal*) is the subject (see 52.13; 53.11); in 53.1-10, a spokesman for the people (the servant?) is the speaker and the suffering figure (i.e., the Lord; see above) is the subject. Further, whereas the suffering figure of 53.1-10 dies, the servant, although marred, lives to become eminent and instruct rulers (see 52.13-15), and to divide spoil (see 53.11-12). In all respects, the latter description points to a Davidic ruler of the last days as the subject: a loyal vassal of the Lord, an individual of whom both Hezekiah and Moses are types, who suffers terribly in his role as proxy for his people's protection, but who lives to spoil 'Assyria' and gain universal eminence (see II, **b. An Entity Synthesis**). In confirmation of this, the Isaianic terms *hand* and *righteous one* (53.10-11) both designate the Davidic ruler, a forerunner of the Lord's coming to reign on the earth (see II, ibid.).

What is significant about the structural contrast of two Israelite kings (the Lord and his vassal[26]) with the king of Babylon is that both account for Israel's redemption, the underlying theme of the Servant-Tyrant Parallelism. The one achieves the temporal deliverance of Israel from a

[24] See Baal, in *ANET*, pp. 139f.; Dumuzi, in Thorkild Jacobsen, *The Treasures of Darkness*, New Haven: Yale, 1976, pp. 25-73.

[25] See the Egyptian and Mesopotamian sun-god as a type of the king, Frankfort, op. cit., pp. 148-61; 307-09.

[26] The Davidic vassal of the Lord is nevertheless himself a suzerain of the kings of the earth, as were David and Solomon, his types (see 1 Kings 4.21, 24; 8.65).

mortal threat, the other the spiritual salvation of Israel from its sins. The one transforms the ancient Near Eastern pattern of the arrested sacrifice of the king, the other the idea of a god whose death is linked to the welfare of the people.[27] Their character in both instances is messianic, the actions and attributes of the one reflecting those of the other, allowing for an overlapping of their description. Notwithstanding their distinct nature and status, both suffer and both redeem, both incur degradation and both are exalted as kings, and both are types of their people. For, in the Prologue of the Servant-Tyrant Parallelism (14.1-3; 47.1-4), Israel also first incurs degradation, but at its redemption is exalted from the dust. It is by virtue of the suffering figure's atonement for sin, however, the key idea of the Servant-Tyrant Parallelism, that all else follows.

c. The End from the Beginning. The broad structuring of the Book of Isaiah to comprehend both Israel's ancient past and its glorious future is essentially that of apocalyptic literature. Typically, apocalyptic works begin with Israel's contemporary woes in the world, amidst which a faithful few look for meaning. Earnest appeals to Israel's God by one who represents the more righteous part of the people are answered by a cosmic vision of the end from the beginning. The visionary is then commanded to write down his vision but to seal up the book to come forth in the last days, the time of its fulfillment.[28] In the Book of Isaiah, each literary structure discussed above commences with historical events contemporary with the age of Isaiah, but each bridges the gap to the last days, the time of Israel's redemption at the coming of its God. This does away with doubts about the eschatological relevance of the Book of Isaiah and repudiates a purely historical view of the book held by some scholars.[29] Moreover, it puts in perspective the futuristic viewpoint variously expressed in all parts of the book, both in its purely

[27] See, respectively, Theodore Gaster, *Thespis: Ritual, Myth and Drama in the Ancient Near East*, New York: Schuman, 1950, pp. 32-43, et al., and *ANET*, p. 68; J. G. Frazer, *Adonis, Attis, Osiris*, New York: Macmillan, 1906; Frankfort, op. cit., pp. 281-94; Jacobsen, op. cit.; *Toward the Image of Tammuz*, Cambridge, Mass.: Harvard, 1970, pp. 73-101.

[28] See the apocalyptic works 1 Enoch, the Assumption of Moses, 2 Baruch, 4 Ezra and Psalms of Solomon in R. H. Charles, *The Apocrypha and Pseudepigrapha, Vol. II*, Oxford: Clarendon, 1963.

[29] See especially the works of Christopher R. North, *The Second Isaiah*, Oxford: Clarendon, 1964; Claus Westermann, *Isaiah 40-66*, Philadelphia: Westminster, 1969; John L. McKenzie, *Second Isaiah*, New York: Doubleday, 1968.

eschatological content and in content made up of historical and non-historical elements (see II, A Message of Content).

Further, the synthesis of the last five structures discussed above, each superimposed upon the intricate Bifid structure, excludes the possibility that the Book of Isaiah is the work of numerous hands. A literary phenomenon such as the above structural synthesis has no known parallel and suggests that the text in its final form is the work of one individual of extraordinary vision. This brings into focus the real prophetic nature of the Book of Isaiah, not limiting it to mere 'historical reflections,' nor even to predictions of things confined to a particular age.

Claims abound of a visionary experience by Isaiah himself of the kind attributed to apocalyptic writers.[30] At least two very ancient traditions of an apocalyptic vision by Isaiah assert that Isaiah saw the end from the beginning. The 'Ascension of Isaiah' speaks of a vision by Isaiah of 'the end of the world,' to be fulfilled 'in the last generation' (Asc. Isa. 11.37-38), a vision he had 'in the twentieth year of the reign of Hezekiah, king of Judah' (Asc. Isa. 1.5-6; 6.1). The book claims that it was 'on account of these visions and prophecies [that] Sammael Satan sawed asunder Isaiah the son of Amoz by the hand of [King] Manasseh' after Hezekiah's death (Asc. Isa. 11.41). It moreover states that 'Beliar[31] harboured great wrath against Isaiah on account of the vision and exposure with which he had exposed Sammael,[32] and because through [Isaiah] the coming forth of the Beloved from the seventh heaven had been revealed' (Asc. Isa. 3.13; cf. 5.15-16). A leading accusation thus brought against Isaiah by the false prophet Belchira was that Isaiah himself had said, 'I see more than the prophet Moses' (Asc. Isa. 3.8). In a similar vein, the writer Ben Sirach claimed that Isaiah saw in vision 'the last things,' revealing 'what would occur to the end of time.' The following passage is from Sirach 48:

[30] As a prophet, none is considered greater in Jewish tradition; see Louis Ginzberg, *Legends of the Jews*, Philadelphia: Jewish Publication Society, 1967, IV:263; VI:375; William G. Braude and Israel J. Kapstein, *Pesikta de-Rab Kahana*, Philadelphia: Jewish Publication Society, 1975, p. 291.

[31] The name *Beliar*, the Greek version of *Belial* (cf. 1 Sam. 25.17, 25; 1 Kings 21.10, 13, etc.), appears to derive from the compound of Heb. *bal, not,* or *běli, without,* and *yaʿal, ascending,* thus denoting *one who cannot ascend* (cf. the emphasis on ascent to heaven, Asc. Isa. 2.9; 7-11, and the king of Babylon's failure to ascend, Isa. 14.12-15).

[32] The names Sammael, Satan, Beliar, etc., appear to be used interchangeably in the 'Ascension' to denote a single figure, a Tyrant king who rules the world in the last days, but who is thrust down to hell (see Asc. Isa. 4.1-14 and the Servant-Tyrant Parallelism, above).

187

²²For Hezekiah did that which pleased the Lord,
    and held fast to the ways of his father David,
    as commanded by Isaiah,
    who was eminently loyal to his vision.

²³In his days the sun reversed,
    and he prolonged the life of the king.

²⁴By the spirit of power he saw the last things,
    and comforted those who mourn in Zion.

²⁵He revealed what would occur to the end of time,
    hidden things, before they transpired.

Ben Sirach's chronological presentation of his material suggests that verses 22 and 23 pertain to the early part of the Book of Isaiah (esp. chs. 9-39) and verses 24 and 25 to the latter part of the book (chs. 40-66). His comment on a *vision* to which Isaiah was loyal (vs. 22) suggests Isaiah's inaugural vision, at which he received his call as a prophet (Isa. 6). The comforting of the mourners in Zion (vs. 24), on the other hand, is a theme of later Isaianic prophecies (see 61.2-3; cf. 40.1; 49.13, etc.). Ben Sirach's parallel structuring of verses 24 and 25 further suggests that 'those who mourn in Zion' (vs. 24b) are comforted *by* the 'hidden things' revealed to Isaiah (vs. 25b), an idea common to apocalyptic literature.³³ The implication of a major vision by Isaiah of 'the last things' by 'the spirit of power' is thus expressly linked by Ben Sirach to the latter part of the Book of Isaiah, not to its early content.

In parallel sections of the Bifid structure in the Book of Isaiah, there occurs a progression of thought from Isaiah's first commission in the vision of Chapter 6 to a second in Chapter 40. In the first, a seraph declares Isaiah's sins atoned for (6.6, 7); in the second, the prophet is to declare Israel's sins atoned for (40.2, 6). In the first, the Lord appears only to Isaiah (6.1, 5); in the second, the Lord is to appear to Israel and to all men (40.5, 9). In the first, the Lord appears on a throne in a cultic setting (6.1); in the second, the setting of his throne is the cosmos (40.22). In effect, the revelation at the foot of the mount, symbolized by the cult (ch. 6), has given way to the revelation on top of the mount, symbolized by the cosmos (ch.40). A cosmic content in Chapter 40, unparalleled in biblical literature, amplifies the cosmic hymn of the seraphs in 6.3. The view is not from below, but from above (40.12, 15, 22, 31); and in that respect it resembles the visions of the apocalyptists. Although the em-

³³See 1 En. 82.1-3; 2 Bar. 81.1-4; 4 Ezr. 6.30-33; 13.53b-56.

phasis on seeing heavenly beings in Chapter 6 and on hearing heavenly beings in Chapter 40 may be a structural device, it is doubtful that in Chapter 40 merely hearing is implied, there being no biblical precedent for heavenly *voices* (40.3, 6) without an accompanying vision.[34] It is more likely that a vision by the prophet is responsible for the cosmic content of Chapter 40 and for the futuristic view and broadened perspective of subsequent writings. In effect, only a vision of the end from the beginning could account for the bold structuring of the Book of Isaiah according to a master plan of composition that emphasizes both the origins and the outcome of Israel's life drama. In the book, the proof repeatedly given of the Lord's divinity is that he alone can make known and has made known the future in the past (see 41.21-26; 43.9-12; 45.19-22, etc.). Without the structural keys that identify this characteristic of the Book of Isaiah with an apocalyptic view of *the end from the beginning* (46.10; cf. 37.26), it must remain, to all intents, a *sealed book* (29.11). When these keys are applied, the work, although written anciently, is seen to address itself particularly to the last days (see 30.8) and to warrant, in the apocalyptic sense, its singular title of a *vision* (1.1).

PART TWO: A MESSAGE OF CONTENT

a. A Synthesis of Events. Besides a structural synthesis, three other syntheses in the Book of Isaiah characterize it as apocalyptic. The first of these, a Synthesis of Events, is a literary device which gives the form of the ancient events of biblical history to prophecies of new events. The new things prophesied are patterned after the old, the one a type of the other. Prominent among these is the Sinai cycle of the Egyptian Bondage, the Passover, the Exodus under Moses, the Lord's Protective Pillar, his Descent on the Mount, the Sinai Covenant, the Lord's Consuming Fire, the Wandering in the Wilderness, the Covenant with Pinehas and the Conquest of the Land under Joshua.[35] By identifying the New Exodus in the Book of Isaiah with the Jews' return from Babylon, scholars have failed to note that the New Exodus is but part of an entire sequence

---

[34] See Isa. 6.1-11; Ezek. 1.1-28; 10.1-22; Dan. 8.16; 10.1-21.

[35] See the Egyptian Bondage, 10.24; 52.4; cf. Exod. 1.8-14; the Passover, 31.5; cf. Exod. 12.27; the Exodus out of Egypt, 11.15-16; 43.2, 16; 51.10; 52.11-12; 58.8; 63.11-14; cf. Exod. 14.15-31; the Lord's Protective Pillar, 4.5-6; 52.12; 58.8; cf. Exod. 14.19-20, 24; the

modeled upon the ancient type, in which all the major events of biblical history are represented. This includes the Chaos[36] preceding the Creation,[37] Paradise, the Cosmic Cataclysm associated with the Flood, the Covenant after the Flood, the Tower of Babel, the Call of Abraham, the Covenant with Abraham, Lot's Escape and the Destruction of Sodom and Gomorrah,[38] and the post-Sinaitic events of the Reign of the Judges, the Victory over Midian, the Davidic Monarchy, the Covenant with David and the Establishment of Zion as the Lord's Residence.[39] It further includes certain events that occurred in the time of Isaiah and beyond, namely, Israel's Apostasy, the Assyrian Invasion, Assyrian Hegemony, the Assyrian Siege, Zion's Deliverance, the Babylonian Captivity, Cyrus' Military Victory and the Rebuilding of Jerusalem.[40]

The sequence of 'new' events based on these types does not, of course, follow the biblical order. They are rearranged and schematized in the Book of Isaiah according to their relationship with one another within

Descent on the Mount, 2.10, 19, 21; 24.23; 29.6; 30.27-28, 30-31; 31.4; 33.3, 10; 64.1-3; 66.15; Exod. 19.16-20; 20.18-20; the Sinai Covenant, 51.16; 54.5; 56.4, 6; cf. Exod. 24.3-8; the Lord's Consuming Fire, 10.16-17; 30.27-28, 33; 31.8-9; 66.15-16, 24; cf. Lev. 10.2; Num. 11.1; the Wandering in the Wilderness, 7.21-25; 40.3-4; 42.16; 43.19-20; 48.21; 49.9-11; 55.12-13; cf. Num. 14.33; the Levitical Covenant, 44.3; 54.13; 59.21; cf. Num. 25.12-13; the Conquest, 11.14; 41.2, 15-16; 45.1-2; 49.17; 54.2-3; cf. Josh. 12.1-24.

[36] Chaos motifs in the Book of Isaiah include darkness, clouds, dust, refuse, chaff, smoke, fire, ashes, water, mud, etc.

[37] See especially 51.16; 65.17-18; 66.22; cf. Gen. 1.1-2.4.

[38] See Paradise, 11.6-9; 35.1-2; 41.18-19; 44.4; 51.3; 55.13; 60.13; 65.25; cf. Gen. 2.8-10, 19-20; Cosmic Cataclysm, 13.9-10, 13; 24.19-21; 34.4; 42.15; 50.2-3; 51.6; 54.10; 64.1; cf. Gen. 7.11; the Flood, 8.7-8; 28.2, 17; 54.9; cf. Gen. 7.10-24; the Covenant after the Flood, 54.9-10; cf. Gen. 9.8-17; the Tower of Babel, 2.15; 30.25; cf. Gen. 11.4; the Call of Abraham, 41.8-9; cf. Gen. 12.1-5; the Covenant with Abraham, 51.2-3; cf. Gen. 15.1-21; 17.1-21; Lot's Escape, 33.14-16; 48.20; 57.1; cf. Gen. 19.12-23, 29; the Destruction of Sodom and Gomorrah, 1.10; 3.9; 9.18-19; 13.9, 19; 32.19; 33.12, 14; 34.4-10; 47.14; cf. Gen. 19.24-26.

[39] See the Reign of the Judges, 1.26; 32.1; cf. Judg. 2.16, 18; the Victory over Midian, 9.4; 10.26; cf. Judg. 7.19-8.12; the Davidic Monarchy, 9.2-7; 11.1-5; 16.5; 32.1; 55.4; cf. 1 Sam. 16.13; 2 Sam. 5.3; Psa. 89.19-20; the Covenant with David, 55.3; cf. 2 Sam. 7.11-16; Psa. 89. 3-4, 26-37; 132.11-12, 18; the Establishment of Zion as the Lord's Residence, 8.18; 12.6; 14.32; 18.7; 24.23; 30.27, 29; 52.8; 59.19-20; 60.9; cf. Deut. 12.5-14; Psa. 132.13-14.

[40] See Israel's Apostasy, esp. 1.2-4; 5.25; 24.5; 57.3-12; the Assyrian Invasion, 5.26-30; 8.8; 10.7-11, 28-32; 36.1; Assyrian Hegemony, 10.5-6, 24; 14.25; 52.4; the Assyrian Siege, 36.1-2; 37.24-29; Zion's Deliverance, 37.32-36; the Babylonian Captivity, 13.3; 38.6-7; 47.6; 52.5; Cyrus' Victory, 41.2-3, 25; 45.1-2; the Rebuilding of Jerusalem, 44.26, 28; 45.13.

the book's eschatological setting, a setting uncovered by its literary structure. The theme of Israel's Return, for example, is nowhere explicitly connected in the Book of Isaiah with Babylon or with the Jews alone, although historically many Jews did return from Babylon. Rather, the Isaianic Return,[41] both of Israel and of Judah, is from the four directions, from many nations and countries, and is connected with the restoration of the law and word of prophecy in the eschatological age (see below). Moreover, the two main actors in this drama of the last days are the Tyrant king and Davidic king, a New David and Goliath. It is the Tyrant, for example, who launches a New Flood of fire upon the earth, an event synonymous with a New Destruction of Sodom and Gomorrah, Cosmic Upheaval and universal Chaos. On the other hand, it is the Davidic ruler who leads the New Exodus out of Babylon before destruction comes, as well as the New Wandering in the Wilderness, the Return of Israel to the Land and the New Conquest (see **b. An Entity Synthesis**). It is the Tyrant who gains the whole world by military force and lays siege to Zion, but whose forces are overthrown at the Lord's New Descent on the Mount at his coming. Again, it is the Davidic ruler who calls Israel home, who regains the world in a succession of military victories, and who rebuilds Jerusalem and its temple for the Lord (ibid.).

Although the use of these types as a literary framework resulted in prophecies that in some ways reflect the historical situation of Isaiah's age, this could only be expected. It validates to a degree the historical relevance of many Isaianic prophecies. It also reflects the universal relevance of the ancient types to diverse situations in space and time. However, the schematization of these types into a sequence that subordinates history overshadows the relevance of Isaianic prophecies to their own age or to any other age to which the prophecies could be likened. It is the very recurrence of these types in a new sequence that characterizes the last days: the last days begin when the sequence of 'new' events is set in motion; they end with a New Creation of Israel and of the earth, an event that consummates and encapsulates the entire sequence. In short, the last days *are* this sequence, a synthesis of new events patterned after the old.

Within this Isaianic schematization of types, no event occurs in isolation from others. All interconnect by key words and motifs, rendering the book's content a unified whole. As an instance of this, the passage in 2.2-5 that deals with the restoration of the law and word of prophecy makes no mention of Israel's Return from its dispersion. Yet key

[41] See 10.20-22; 11.10-12; 14.1-2; 35.10; 43.5-6; 49.12, 18, 22; 51.11; 56.8; 60.4; 66.20.

terms and motifs in each of its verses relate the passage to Israel's Return in various other contexts in the Book of Isaiah. In verse 2, the verb *flow* or *stream* (Heb. *nāhărû*) characterizes *nations* or *Gentiles* (Heb. *gôyîm*) streaming to Zion. The question arises why the term *flow* is used in preference to a more common one, such as *go* or *come*. It is that the term *flow* and the idea of *nations* streaming to Zion occur in other, related contexts in the Book of Isaiah. In 60.5 and 66.12, these Hebrew terms coincide in a context of Israel's Return, but without any time identification such as that of *the latter days* in 2.2. This rhetorical correlation of content accomplishes two things. First, it identifies the streaming of the nations to Zion in 2.2 with Israel's Return, an idea not explicit in that verse; second, it identifies the Return in 60.5 and 66.12 with the latter days, an idea not stated there. Likewise, verse 3 of the restoration passage links rhetorically to Israel's Return. Here, the verb *go up* (Heb. *naʿăleh*) is a pilgrimage motif and a key word. Several times a year, in the seasons of religious festivals, the ancient Israelites *went up* to Zion/Jerusalem from throughout the Land to make a pilgrimage to the temple of the Lord (see Psa. 122.1-4). The Israelite pilgrimage, made in remembrance of the cycle of events associated with Sinai, became a prophetic type of Israel's Return from throughout the earth (see Jer. 31.6), and its imagery is used in that context in 30.29; 35.8-10; 51.10-11. By means of the verb *go up*, the idea of Israel's Return is thus again related to the scene of the nations going to Zion in 2.3, and the Return itself with a latter-day setting.

In the next two verses, which describe a second phase of Israel's restoration, the term *judge* (Heb. *šāpaṭ*) in verse 4 and *light* (Heb. *ʾôr*) in verse 5 also relate the passage to Israel's Return. The term *judge* occurs rhetorically in 11.3-4; 16.5; 51.5 in a context in which Israel's Return has taken place and its king reigns, while the term *light* is linked to a scene of Israel's Return from throughout the earth in 60.1-4. There the *light* is the glory of the Lord which attracts nations and rulers, sons and daughters to Zion. In 51.4, the *light* is the law itself, going forth to all nations; and in yet other contexts it is a metaphor for the Davidic king, who calls Israel home (see **b. An Entity Synthesis**). The entire restoration passage of 2.2-5 thus has to do with Israel's Return *in the latter days* (2.2). However, the time identification *in the latter days* occurs only here in the entire text, leaving it an open question in passages dealing explicitly with Israel's Return when the event is to take place. The question is resolved when a rhetorical relationship is perceived between events linked by a key word or motif. The above relationship, for example, does away with the necessity seen by scholars for interpreting Israel's Return in the Book of Isaiah to be the Jews' historical return from Babylon, and the subsequent restriction of a large part of Isaianic prophecies to the remote past. For closely related to the event of Israel's Return, as represented throughout the Book of Isaiah, are other major events in the above sequence of types, all of which thus relate to *the latter days.*

The inclusion of events of Isaiah's own age among types forming an eschatological sequence merits special attention. Prophecies connected with the names of world powers whose activities were only newly happening, such as Babylon, Assyria and Egypt, serve a classic dual function, one historical, the other eschatological. The historical relevance of such prophecies is an obvious one, making up the bulk of present commentaries on the Book of Isaiah and therefore requiring little clarification here. Isaiah's age, however, represented a turning point in ancient Near Eastern history, a time when historical precedents occurred which formed types as valid as any precedents before them. In the Book of Isaiah, it is precisely the precedental nature of a major biblical event that qualifies it as a type of the future. This does not mean that any Isaianic prophecy, as first uttered or written, was simultaneously applicable to its own time and to the time of the end, but that a change in emphasis occurred from the former to the latter. This change in emphasis, given impetus by a broad vision of the end from the beginning that governs the book's structure, provided the motivation for the systematic editing and schematization of Isaianic prophecies into their final complex and sophisticated form. The integration of newly written material with an existing collection of prophetic oracles followed a single plan whose correlation of types and rhetoric achieved horizontally what the book's structural layers achieved vertically. Structure and content, each in its own way, thus formed a synthesis—a synthesis that characterizes the Book of Isaiah not merely as eschatological, because it relates to the last days, but as apocalyptic, because it sets forth a total vision of the last days.

It is not surprising, then, that many of the 'new' events in the Isaianic synthesis should reappear in the apocalyptic literature itself.[42] Even the post-Exilic prophets still predicted a 'great and dreadful day of the Lord'

[42] See Apostasy, 1 En. 91.6-7; 93.9; 99.6-9; 2 Bar. 48.38, 40; Invasion of the Land, 1 En. 56.6; 57.1-2; 4 Ezr. 13.5, 8; Psa. Sol. 2.20; Universal Judgment by Fire, 1 En. 91.8-9; 100.9; 102.1; Ass. Mos. 10.10; 2 Bar. 27.10; 48.39; 53.7; 70.8; 1QH5; 1QH10; 1QH23; Cosmic Cataclysm, 1 En. 1.6-7; 60.1; 83.3-4; Ass. Mos. 10:4-6; 2 Bar. 27.7; 70.8; 4 Ezr. 3.18-19; 9.3; 13.2-4; 1QH5; 1QH23; Israel's Return, 4 Ezr. 13.39-40; Psa. Sol. 11.1-7; 17.34, 50; the Descensus, 1 En. 1.3-5; Ass. Mos. 10.3-4, 7; the Covenant, 1 En. 1.8; 60.6; Psa. Sol. 11.8c-9; 1QH23; Rebuilding of the Temple, 1 En. 90.28-29; 2 Bar. 32.4; a New Creation, 1 En. 45.

(Mal. 4.1-5), a Cosmic Cataclysm (Hag. 2.6-7, 21), a Flood (Dan. 11.40), an Exodus (Zech. 10.11), a Descensus (Zech. 9.14), and a Return of greater Israel (Zech. 2.11; 8.7-8, 20-22; Tobit 14.5). However, owing to the historical origins of much of the book's content, their eschatological intent remains for the most part implicit; the book's latter-day relevance as a whole is recoverable only by the literary keys discussed above. The eschatological intent of the apocalyptic works, on the other hand, is explicit throughout; descriptions of visions of the last days are generally not couched in historical terms. All that is eschatological in the apocalyptic works is nevertheless represented in the Book of Isaiah, where the picture of the last days is all-inclusive. No latter-day event appears in the apocalyptic works that does not appear in the Book of Isaiah, though the reverse is not the case. Because of its totality or *sum of vision* (29.11; 48.6), the Book of Isaiah is thus a work of apocalyptic literature superior to any of the apocalyptic genre, and it should be read as such. In the one, syntheses of events that depict the last days appear isolated and fragmented;[43] in the other, the synthesis of events is cohesive and complete. In the one, the structure of a work is somewhat arbitrary and obscure; in the other, the structure is predetermined and clearly discernible. It follows that only as an apocalyptic work does the Book of Isaiah fully make sense, leaving nothing unexplained or unaccounted for.

b. An Entity Synthesis. A common error of scholars is to interpret prophecies about figures or entities featured in the Book of Isaiah on the basis of historical facts. The only valid basis for interpreting such prophecies, however, is not to read into them historical data, but simply to view the book's entities as they appear in the text; what matters is not the historical facts surrounding Isaianic entities, but the way they are characterized in the book. The characterization of Isaianic entities, which centers on three pairs of major figures, is generally a blend of things historical and things not historical, and consequently its intention is not to depict entities as purely historical. With regard to Assyria, for example, it is significant that the Book of Isaiah deals with an Assyrian Invasion (see 5.24-29; 7.17-20; 8.7-8, etc.) but not with an Assyrian Exile, although both were major events of Isaiah's day. For the theme of Israel's Exile, where apparent in the Book of Isaiah, occurs

4b-5a; Paradise, 1 En. 10.18-19; 2 Bar. 29.5-7; 73.6-74.1; 1QH10. See the Thanksgiving Psalms (1QH) in Geza Vermes, *The Dead Sea Scrolls in English*, Baltimore: Penguin Books, 1962.

[43] See, for example, 1 En. 1.3-9; 45.4-6; 50.1-51.1; 60.5-6; 91.5-10; Ass. Mos. 10.3-10; 2 Bar. 29.5-30.5; 32.1-6; 48.31-40; 4 Ezr. 13.2-13; Psa. Sol. 11.1-9.

throughout as a presupposition, being nowhere explicitly predicted. Moreover, whereas the Assyrian Invasion of Israel represented a historical precedent, thus qualifying it as a type for the last days (see **a. A Synthesis of Events**), an Assyrian Exile did not; Israel had been removed from its Land before, in Egypt. The characterization of Assyria, however, is not merely selective in its use of historical facts, but adds things ahistorical, things having no historical basis at all: Assyria, a major world power of Isaiah's time, is depicted as overthrown in battle 'in my own land' (14.25), 'as in the day of Midian' (9.4; 10.26; cf. Judg. 7.15-8.13), 'fought in mortal combat' (30.32) and defeated with 'a sword not of men' (31.8). The Isaianic 'Assyria,' therefore, is not a purely historical Assyria, although it bears some of that nation's typological traits. It is an entity that is synthesized to serve a higher, eschatological purpose, an entity whose activities as a world power of the last days resemble, in many respects, those of its historical type.

Similarly, Egypt is characterized in the Book of Isaiah as a politically blundering world power (see 19.12-15), as a victim of defeat (31.3) and, for a time, of foreign rule (19.4)—that of Assyria (see 20.4; 31.3, 8; 37.25). These things reflect historical realities. Having no historical basis, however, is the coming of the Lord to Egypt (see 19.1), the conversion of the Egyptians to the Lord (19.21-22), and their deliverance from subjection by a *savior* sent by the Lord (19.20); and one must therefore look beyond history for an interpretation of the Isaianic 'Egypt.' In short, it is this synthesis of historical and ahistorical elements that lifts Isaianic entities from the realm of history to that of eschatology. One may emphasize historical elements, and thus the relevance of Isaianic entities to their historical setting; but where such elements form part of Isaianic syntheses, as most do, they are valid mainly as types. The names of historical entities in that case serve as codenames for eschatological ones, the one entity a type of the other. Needless to say, this is in harmony with the structural and typological syntheses discussed above, as well as with the nature of apocalyptic literature.

The characterization of Isaianic entities includes their contrast or juxtaposition in pairs. Assyria and Egypt, Babylon and Zion, the Tyrant king and the Davidic king—each pair of major entities is set in opposition, both structurally and typologically. Assyria, for example, is cast in the political role of invader and world conqueror (see 36.1, 19-20; 37.11-13, 24-25), while Egypt is looked to as a refuge and source of protection against Assyria by the weaker nations of the world (see 20.5-6; 30.1-2; 36.6). Historically, it was these traits which constituted biblical precedents, thus validating Assyria and Egypt as political types. Assyria was the first power to conquer the entire ancient world by military force, while Egypt, the greatest world power up to that time, exemplified an 'arm of flesh' on which men were tempted to rely. Egypt's vast force of men and chariots (31.1) seemed a logical alternative to the much less logical idea of divine protection against Assyria (see 30.15, 27-32; 31.4-5, 8-9).

Babylon, on the other hand, though historically following in Assyria's footsteps as a military world power, was most notorious for its idolatry; and only in that respect, therefore, does it serve as a biblical type: in the Book of Isaiah, Assyria is represented as a physical power of Chaos (see 5.25, 30; 8.7-8; 10.6, etc.),[44] while Babylon represents spiritual chaos, or Apostasy (see 46.1-2; 47.10, 12-13). Babylon's domination of the world takes the form of an idolatrous materialism (see 40.19-20; 44.9-20; 46.6-7), and within the Bifid structure Babylon has as its mercantile aspect, Tyre. Both Tyre and Babylon, moreover, are characterized as a harlot or mistress of the kingdoms of the world (see 23.3, 11-12, 16; 47.5, 7-8), bereft of children in the day of Judgment (see 14.22; 23.4; 47.9), and punished by physical violence (see 21.9; 23.1, 11; 47.11, 14). An ahistorical element in the Isaianic characterization of Babylon is its overthrow in a New Sodom and Gomorrah Destruction (13.19; 47.14), never to be reinhabited (13.20-22; 47.1, 5). While idolatry, or spiritual Chaos, in the Book of Isaiah is thus punished physically, militarism, in the form of physical Chaos, is punished by means of divine, or spiritual power (see 10.16-18; 30.30-33; 31.8-9). The deliverance of Zion/Jerusalem from Assyria is similarly by divine intervention (see I. **b. A Structural Synthesis**).

The characterization of entities as syntheses in the Book of Isaiah—influenced by a prophetic vision which looks beyond the historical reality to the eschatological type—is not limited to non-Israelite nations. The Isaianic Zion, too, is a synthesis of historical and ahistorical elements. In the Isaianic schematization of events, Jerusalem/Zion is created out of the universal Chaos that ensues in the day of Judgment (see 14.31-32; 27.12-13; 30.28-29, etc.), a rebirth that is synonymous with the New Creation of the earth itself (see 51.16; 65.17-18; 66.22). As a synthesis, Zion is contrasted with Babylon. This is most apparent in the prologue of the Servant-Tyrant Parallelism, where Babylon is dethroned, disrobed and banished into the dust by Zion's Redeemer (47.1-4), while Zion is called from the dust, clad in priestly robes and enthroned as part of its redemption by the Lord (52.1-3). Just as there is a Zion ideology in the Book of Isaiah, so there is a Babylon 'ideology':

---

[44] See footnotes 6 and 36.

Babylon represents all that Zion is not, and vice versa. Babylon is destroyed (see above) and Zion delivered (see I, **b. A Structural Synthesis**); Babylon's gods are taken captive, unable to save Babylon (46.1-2), while Israel's God grants deliverance in Zion (46.13). Babylon is a harlot (see above), Zion a (now) faithful wife (54.5; 62.4-5); Babylon is bereft of children (see above), while Zion's children return and are born (60.4-9; 66.7-8). Covenant curses befall Babylon (13.19-22; 47.11); covenant blessings and curse reversals befall Zion (see **c. A Covenant Synthesis**). Not surprisingly, this contrast of Babylon and Zion in the Book of Isaiah carries over into the apocalyptic literature itself.[45]

Each of the four Isaianic syntheses, Assyria and Egypt, Babylon and Zion, represents both a people and a place. The Assyrians and their allies are depicted as predators (5.29; 10.6; 33.4, 18), aroused to anger (5.30; 10.5; 17.12), insolent (33.19; 36.12-14; 37.6), politically treacherous (33.1, 8), militarily intrusive (8.7-8; 18.2; 37.11), universally destructive (10.7-11; 36.10; 37.18) and oppressive in their rule (10.24, 27; 14.25; 30.31). Assyria's land is 'the North' (14.31). The Egyptians, on the other hand, are political blunderers (19.11-14), a declining world power (19.15; 31.3), a great military power (30.2; 31.1) allied with other nations (30.1, 4; 31.2-3), a fearful people (19.16-17) socially divided (19.2), wicked and idolatrous (19.1, 3; 31.2), in part religious (19.18-21), but no match for Assyria in a confrontation (20.5-6; 30.5, 7; 31.3). As a country, Egypt is industrial (19.9-10) and its land lush (19.5-7).

In the pair Babylon-Zion, Babylon is characterized as a shipping empire (23.13; 43.14), a merchandizing society (47.15), technological (47.10), sophisticated (13.19), refined (47.1, 8), palatial (13.22) idolatrous (21.9; 47.13), wicked (47.10) and oppressive (21.2; 47.6). In a prophecy addressed to Babylon (see 13.1), the people Babylon are defined by context as *sinners* (13.9) and *the wicked* (13.11), while the place Babylon is identified as *the earth* (13.5, 9, 13) and *the world* (13.11). On the other hand, Zion as a people is defined by parallelism[46] as those of Israel who repent (see 1.27; 59.20); Zion as a place is identified by context as the rendezvous of those who are ransomed, or redeemed (35.10; 51.11). Those of Israel who *return* home (Heb. *šûb*) are those of Israel who *repent* of idolatry (Heb. *šûb*), while others are destroyed in the world

---

[45] See 2 Bar. 11.1-2; 13.3-10; 4 Ezr. 3.2.

[46] I.e., by means of the parallel structuring of verses (italics mine):

Zion shall be ransomed by justice,	He will come as Redeemer to *Zion*,
those of her who repent by righteousness.	to *those of Jacob who repent of trans-*
(1.27)	*gression*, says the Lord. (59.20)

197

at large, or 'Babylon' (see 10.21-23; 27.9, 12-13; 51.7, 11-14). Just as historical Israel was born as a nation at the Exodus out of Egypt, so eschatological Israel, or 'Zion,' is born as a nation at the New Exodus out of Babylon before the latter's destruction (see 48.18-22; 51.9-11; 52.1-3, 11-12).

Within the Bifid structure, Babylon is a synthesis of all nations other than Zion; national entities other than Zion are structurally subsumed under one head, 'Babylon.' A later development of the Babylon-Zion contrast in the Bifid structure is the idea of two *cities*, one wicked (cf. 22. 2; 25.2), the other righteous (cf. 1.26; 52.1; 62.12), one destroyed (cf. 24. 12; 25.2; 32.14), the other delivered (cf. 26.1; 37.33-35; 60.14). Ultimately, this concept develops structurally into only two categories of people who exist on earth, non-Zion and Zion. Each is a synthesis, universal in origin; each is affiliated by formal ties (or a covenant) to one or other political and spiritual power on the earth—there is no provision, structurally, for a middle ground in the last days. Contrasted in the Bifid structure, therefore, are two covenants, a covenant with Death (cf. 28.15, 18), consisting of human *counsel, plans*, etc. (cf. 29.15; 30.1), and a covenant of life (cf. 55.3), personified by the Davidic king (see **c. A Covenant Synthesis**), who serves as a proxy for Zion's deliverance. At the last, within the Bifid structure, there takes place a total separation of people based on their covenantal affiliation.[47] Non-Zion, because it rejects the Lord's restored law and word of prophecy, incurs Chaos in the day of Judgment; Zion, upon demonstrating its rejection of human counsel and its loyalty to the covenant, receives divine protection and attains to kingship and the holy priesthood. Such a view of the last days is the essence of apocalyptic, which is largely made up of ideas of this kind.

The division of Assyria and Egypt, Babylon and Zion, into political and spiritual pairs merges in the Tyrant king and Davidic king: each is both political and spiritual; each king personifies the corporate entity—the people he represents—the one a villain, the other a hero. The two kings, moreover, form syntheses of the major villains and heroes of biblical history. In the case of the Tyrant king, this synthesis results in a kind of arch-villain, one who exemplifies all the worst traits of history's evil rulers; in the case of the Davidic king, the synthesis results in the ideal ruler, one who exemplifies all the best traits of history's heroes.

In the Book of Isaiah, the major villains of the time are represented as

---

[47] This is also evident in the case of 'Edom' (34.5-7), a synthesis of all nations (see 34.1-2; cf. Amos 9.12), which, as a biblical type, denotes covenantal alienation from the Lord (see Gen. 25.30-34; Joel 3.19; Amos 1.9, 11; Obad. 11-14).

the kings of Assyria and Babylon. Both kings assume militaristic as well as idolatrous traits: both come from the north (see 10.28-32; 14.13, 31), are hewers of the cedars of Lebanon (see 10.15, 33-34; 14.8; 37.24)[48] and conquerors of the whole earth (see 10.12-14; 14.5-7, 21), and as the Lord's rivals (see 14.13-14; 37.10-12, 23-29), they impose the yoke of servitude on his people (see 10.24, 27; 14.3-5, 25). Both kings are political, personifying the militaristic traits of Isaiah's Assyria, and, as mythologized demigods, they are spiritual in the sense that they personify the idolatry of the Isaianic Babylon. As syntheses, both are characterized as ahistorical as well as historical, corresponding to their respective mythologized and real portrayals (see 10.5-34; 14.3-20; 36.1-37.38). Both kings exemplify an arch-Tyrant who, when his work is done, is punished by the Lord for his presumptuousness (see 10.12-15; 14.12-20; 37.26-29). In short, unlike Assyria and Babylon themselves, they are two halves of the same coin, comprising one and the same instrument of the Lord's wrath in the *day* of Judgment;[49] their typological merger as one archetype further accords with the eschatological setting of the Book of Isaiah discussed previously. Structurally contrasted with the arch-Tyrant is the Davidic king, his contemporary, who is a synthesis of the biblical heroes, Abraham, Moses, Joshua, Gideon, David, Solomon and Cyrus. This synthesis appears in two parallel sections of the Bifid structure.[50] In the first section (chs. 9-12), the Davidic king, who features prominently in Chapters 9, 11-12, is contrasted structurally with the Tyrant king in Chapter 10. This contrast with the Tyrant king carries over into a series of alternating themes of Chaos and Creation which begins earlier than the section, but climaxes in it.[51] Within these contrasting structures, the Davidic king appears as a power of Creation[52] that ultimately vanquishes the powers of Chaos represented by the Tyrant king. Certain metaphors which emphasize these creative and chaotic powers are used

[48] See the mythological connotation of this motif in *ANET*, p. 79. In the Book of Isaiah, as elsewhere in the Bible, 'Lebanon' is a figure for Israel (see Isa. 2.13; 14.8; 33.9; Deut. 3.25; Judg. 9.15; 2 Kings 14.9; Psa. 104.16).

[49] Within the eschatological setting of the Book of Isaiah, the word *day* runs like a thread throughout the text, a lexical reminder of but a single stage of events. In the present context, see the term in 7.17, 20; 10.3, 17, 27; 13.6, 9, 13; 14.3.

[50] Viz., that whose subject is Agents of Divine Deliverance and Judgment: chs. 9-12; 41-46.

[51] See footnote 9.

[52] In harmony with royal theology of the ancient Near East; see Frankfort, op. cit., pp. 150f.; Walter Brueggemann, 'Kingship and Chaos,' *CBQ*, 33 (1971), pp. 317-32.

overtly in Chapters 9-12 to depict the two kings. The use of metaphors representing the two kings nevertheless extends to the entire Book of Isaiah, although elsewhere in the text their use is generally not overt. In other words, the various terms employed as metaphors appear throughout the book, but for the most part it is left to the reader to recognize them as such.

For example, in 11.10-16 the Davidic king (the *sprig of Jesse*, verse 10) is identified as an *ensign* which attracts *nations* or *Gentiles*. In verse 12, however, whose theme is Israel's Return, the *nations* rallied by the ensign are identified as Israel and Judah. Also in verse 12, the term *ensign* is structurally paralleled with the Lord's *hand* in verse 11, indicating a synonymous relationship between the two terms (see this also in 49.22). The term *hand* further appears in verse 14, whose theme is a New Conquest, and in verse 15, whose theme is a New Exodus. In each case, its primary function is that of a power to accomplish the Lord's creative purpose; its secondary function nevertheless remains that of a metaphor representing the Davidic king,[53] the instrument used by the Lord to accomplish this purpose. For anciently, it was Moses who led the Exodus, Joshua who led the Conquest, and David who united Judah and Ephraim (see verse 13), another theme of the above passage. This passage in the Book of Isaiah thus sets forth the mission of the Davidic king, who is to be a New David, Moses and Joshua in the sense that he fulfills all the above roles.

In 10.26, the use of metaphors for the Davidic king extends to the Lord's *whip* (or *scourge*) and *staff*, both royal insignia of the ancient Near East, as is the term *ensign*.[54] The term *whip* occurs in a context of a victory over Assyria patterned after Israel's Victory over Midian, while the term *staff* occurs in a context of a New Exodus. Leading Israel's Victory over Midian anciently, however (see Judg. 7.15-8.13), was Gideon, who, in the same historical context, was styled as one who whipped his enemies with briars and thorns (see Judg. 8.7, 16). The implied role of Moses at the Exodus is more familiar (see Exod. 14.16), but the verse's context, that of a victory over Assyria, affirms that the New Moses is also a New Gideon. Thus the terms *Sea* (Yamm) and *River* (Nahar),[55] which in the above passages represent forces subdued

---

[53] See the Davidic theology of the king as the *man of thy right hand*, Psa. 80.17; 110.1.

[54] See Frankfort, op. cit., p. 200.

[55] Both terms represent ancient Near Eastern powers of Chaos; see *ANET*, pp. 129ff; Herbert G. May, 'Some Cosmic Connotations of *Mayim Rabbim*, "Many Waters,"' *JBL*, 74 (1955), pp. 9-21.

by the Lord's *hand* and *staff* (see 10.26; 11.15), are Isaianic pseudonyms for Assyria (see 5.30; 7.20; 8.7): in each case, it is Assyria that is vanquished, and in each case it is the Davidic king—when the above terms are read as metaphors—who leads the event (see also 30.32; 31.9).

The use of metaphors to represent the Davidic king has a counterpart in the Tyrant king, or their use would not be as significant. The Tyrant king too is represented as a *staff* (see 9.4; 10.24; 14.5), and is identified overtly as such in 10.5, 15. He also appears as a *whip* or *scourge* (see 28. 15, 18), as a *rod* (9.4; 10.5, 15, 24; 30.31),[56] a *yoke* (9.4; 10.27; 14.25), an *axe* and a *saw* (10.15). In every case, he is an instrument of the Lord's punishment of Israel. The Tyrant king further appears under the metaphor *hand*, to denote the Lord's hand of punishment (see 5.25; 10.4-5; 28.2), as well as an *ensign* rallying an alliance of nations against Israel (see 5.26; 13.2). Other less evident metaphors that represent both the Tyrant king and Davidic king include the *voice* (see 13.2; 30.30-31; 31.4), the *tongue* (11.15; 30.27; 35.6), the *breath* or *wind* (11.15; 30.28; 33.11) and the *branch* (11.1; 14.19).[57] Metaphors for the two kings not held in common feature a division of divine attributes: the Tyrant king appears as the Lord's *anger* and *wrath* (see 5.25; 10.4-5, 25; 13.3, 5, 9, 13) and as his *rage*, *fury* and *indignation*, etc. (see 30.27, 30; 34.2); the Davidic king appears as the Lord's *righteousness* or *righteous one* (see 1.25-27; 41.2, 10; 46.13; 51.1, 7),[58] as a *light* (see 9.2; 58.8), and as the Lord's *arm* (see 30.30; 40.10-11; 51.5). In summary, the phenomenon of metaphors shared by the Tyrant king and Davidic king denotes that the two are rivals;[59] the related phenomenon of divergent metaphors, on the other hand, denotes that one of the two kings is divinely sanctioned, the other not. In view of the eschatological setting of the Book of Isaiah within which the above metaphors and events are most meaningful, it is not surprising that a number of them, as well as this latter-day context, should be reflected in the apocalyptic literature.[60]

[56] See a Davidic king as *rod* in 14.29, viz., Ahaz (cf. 14.28).

[57] The term *branch* (Heb. *nēṣer*) has a variety of meanings (see *fetus*, 14.19), mainly emphasizing *offspring*.

[58] See the ancient Near Eastern background of *righteousness* personified in the Davidic king, in Roy A. Rosenberg, 'The God Sedeq,' *HUCA*, 36 (1965), pp. 161-78.

[59] See the ancient Near Eastern background of such arch-rivalry in the contests between Seth and Horus, Yamm and Baal, et al., in Frankfort, op. cit., pp. 21f.; 25f.; *ANET*, pp. 129ff.

[60] See the *righteous one*, 1 En. 38.2; 53.6; Psa. Sol. 17.35-36; a *light* to the righteous, 1 En. 38.2; 48.4; the Davidic king as a *rod*, Psa. Sol. 18.8; the Davidic king as a vassal of the Lord, Psa. Sol. 17.38. *wrath* and a *whip* in the day of Judgment, 1QH5, etc.

The main subjects of the parallel section of the Bifid structure (Chapters 41-46) divide into two, a Servant figure and a Warrior figure. Each is characterized by elements that are ahistorical as well as historical. A classic example of this is Cyrus. Without reading other historical data into the Isaianic Cyrus, we find that this figure is depicted (1) as one who initiates the rebuilding of Jerusalem and its temple (see 44.28; 45.13), and (2) as a universal warrior type, overthrowing nations and rulers as a power for good (see 45.1-2).[61] It is precisely in these two things that the historical Cyrus constitutes a biblical type; by these events Cyrus created important biblical precedents, of relevance as a pattern for the last days (see **a. A Synthesis of Events**). His name, therefore, receives mention in the Book of Isaiah in connection with them. Ahistorical elements characterizing Cyrus are nevertheless of equal significance. In the context in which he appears, Cyrus is also depicted as the Lord's *servant* (44.26), as *my shepherd* (44.28), an idea linked to the theme of a New Exodus (44.27), and as the Lord's *anointed*, invested as king and commissioned by the Lord himself (45.1).[62] The concept of the Lord's *servant* (an ancient Near Eastern synonym for *vassal*) establishes a rhetorical link between Cyrus and the Servant figure, who features prominently in the same section of the Bifid structure (see below). The concept of the Lord's *shepherd*, linked to the theme of a New Exodus, is a Moses typology; the two ideas coincide elsewhere in the Book of Isaiah only in connection with Moses (see 63.11-13). The concept of the Lord's *anointed* is for the most part a David and Solomon typology (see 1 Sam. 16.12; 1 Kings 1.39). The Isaianic 'Cyrus,' therefore, is not a purely historical figure, but a synthesis of Cyrus, the Servant figure, Moses, David and Solomon. Similarly in 45.13, the theme of the rebuilding of Jerusalem, a Cyrus typology, is synthesized with the event of Israel's release, a Moses typology (see Exod. 3.9-10); in 41.2, the call of a righteous figure from the east to the Lord's footstool, an Abraham typology (see Gen. 12.1), is synthesized with the event of one who treads down world authorities, a Cyrus typology (see 45.1-2). In each example, history has been subordinated in the interest of creating an ideal type: a royal Warrior figure called from the East who overthrows rulers and nations while on a march of Conquest, who releases Israel's exiles and rebuilds Jerusalem and its temple after a New Exodus.

---

[61] I.e., in part, in order that the Lord's people might be released from (Babylonian) bondage; see 45.13.

[62] See as royal accession motifs the grasping of the right hand and calling by name (45.1, 3-4) in Shalom M. Paul, 'Deutero-Isaiah and Cuneiform Royal Inscriptions,' *JAOS*, 88 (1968), pp. 180-86.

In the same section of the Bifid structure, the Servant figure of 42.1-7,[63] too, is a synthesis. A parallel with Cyrus is his royal commission by the Lord through the grasping of the hand (42.6; see footnote 62) and his universal mission to the nations (42.1, 4, 6). The Servant's endowment by the Lord's Spirit within the context of a royal commission is a David and Solomon typology (see 1 Sam. 16.13; 1 Kings 3.12); his role as a lawgiver who does not fail in strength (42.4) is a Moses typology (see Deut. 33.4; 34.7). The Servant's setting free of blind captives (42.7), in a context of a New Wandering in the Wilderness (42.16), is in part a Moses typology; his personification of the Lord's covenant (42.6) is in part a Davidic typology (see **c. A Covenant Synthesis**). Since it designates a royal figure, the title *my servant* (42.1) thus expresses a vassal relationship to the Lord; as well as a universal lawgiver, the Servant is a universal ruler whose suzerain is the Lord. On the other hand, the Warrior figure, too, is the Lord's vassal, accounting for the peculiar statement concerning Cyrus: 'he will do whatever I will' (44.28).

Both the Warrior and Servant syntheses in this section, however, personify, in a single individual, the corporate entity Israel. Israel, too, when held by the Lord's *righteous right hand* (41.10), makes chaos of the nations (41.15),[64] as does the Warrior figure (41.2, 25); Israel, too, is called from the end of the earth (41.8-9), as is the Warrior figure (41.2, 25; 46.11). Israel is called by name (43.1), is the Lord's *servant* (41.8-9; 43.10), and is endowed with the Lord's Spirit (44.3), as is the Servant figure (42.1; 49.3). The Warrior and Servant syntheses may thus be seen as two manifestations of a single ideal, an ideal made up of the biblical heroes Abraham, Moses, David, Solomon and Cyrus. This is confirmed within a series of alternating themes of Chaos and Creation that spans this section of the Book of Isaiah;[65] within the chiastic structure into which these themes are arranged, the Warrior and Servant figures complement one another: the spiritual aspect of the ideal is represented by the Servant figure, the political aspect by the Warrior figure. Not surprisingly, this separation of political and spiritual attributes occurs also in the Davidic king, in the parallel section of the Bifid structure (Chapters 9-12). In 9.2-7 the political attributes of the Davidic king are emphasized, in 11.2-5 his spiritual attributes. A progression of thought from

---

[63] The Servant is introduced in 42.1-6, whose chiastic structure (a-b-c-c-b-a) determines that he is its subject throughout. Verse 7 elaborates on his mission.

[64] See the term *mountains* in this verse as Isaianic metaphors for *nations* or *kingdoms* in the parallel structure of 13.4; 64.1-3.

[65] See footnote 9.

the first section (chs. 9-12) to the second (chs. 41-46) is the universalizing of the ideal type: both are syntheses of Abraham,[66] Moses, David and Solomon; but the national warriors Joshua and Gideon in the first section are replaced by Cyrus in the second. Both syntheses, whether represented as *son* (9.6) or *servant* (42.1), are the Lord's vassal; both feature within the same group of metaphors (viz., *light*, 9.2; 42.6; *hand*, 11.11; 41.10, etc.); both are identified with the theme of Creation in parallel series of the Chaos/Creation pattern. Lastly, both appear in a context which emphasizes the typological events of the Return, a New Exodus, a New Wandering in the Wilderness, and a New Conquest.[67] It therefore follows that the two parallel sections of the Bifid structure depict a single ideal figure, who, as a synthesis of the biblical heroes Abraham, Moses, Joshua, Gideon, David, Solomon and Cyrus, is not historical but eschatological; his sphere of action is the last days, the time when the above typological events are fulfilled. The absence of an arch-Tyrant in the second section of the Bifid structure implies that the ideal figure has prevailed over his rival.

Apart from the ideal figure's contrast with and victory over the arch-Tyrant—expressed structurally and typologically in the Book of Isaiah —he features as a forerunner of the coming of the Lord. The Lord's coming to establish his universal rule on the earth occurs as the climax of a long series of typological events that make up the last days (see 59. 19-60.3; 66.18-23). It also occurs locally by divine intervention within the series of typological events itself.[68] The leading figures in these preliminary events, however, are the arch-Tyrant and the ideal Davidic king, of whom one prevails (see above). In the Book of Isaiah, the Davidic king's function as forerunner of the Lord's coming is ideally expressed by means of the metaphors *righteousness* and *salvation*, the first of which designates the Davidic king (see 41.2; 53.11), the second the Lord

---

[66] Abraham, as a type, is represented in the first section of the Bifid structure by the royal title *Wonderful Counsellor, Mighty One of Valor, Father for Ever, Prince of Peace* (9.6). Exemplifying Abraham, as depicted in successive narratives of the Genesis account, are the attributes of counsel, viz., in the dispute with Lot (ch. 13); valor, in the war against the coalition of northern kings (ch. 14); fatherhood, after two tentative heirs (chs. 15-16), Isaac (ch.17); and peacemaker/savior, in his intercession on behalf of the righteous in Sodom (ch. 18; see Lot, Gen. 19.29).

[67] See the Return, 10.21-22; 11.10-12; New Exodus, 11.15-16; 43.2, 16; New Wandering in the Wilderness, 9.2; 42.16; 43.19-20; New Conquest, 11.14; 41.2; 45.1-2.

[68] E.g., at the New Exodus, 52.12; 58.8; a New Passover, 31.5; a New Descent on the Mount, 24.23; 31.4, etc.

himself (see 12.2; 62.11; 63.8).[69] Both the ideal figure and the Lord also appear under the metaphor *arm* (see 33.2; 40.10; 51.5, 9; 53.1), signifying their complementary but not synonymous relationship. According to this relationship, *righteousness* precedes *salvation* (see 46.11-13; 51.5-8). In other words, *salvation* (the Lord) does not come until *righteousness* (the Davidic king) is established among the people Israel; as at Sinai (see Exod. 19.5-11), the suzerain (the Lord) does not appear until his vassal is prepared to meet him. Since both the Davidic king and Israel are the Lord's vassal, the Davidic king's personification of his people finds expression in common titles: both are designated the Lord's *son* (see Exod. 4.22; Isa. 9.6) and *servant* (see Exod. 4.23; Isa. 41.8; 49.3), and both are named *Israel* (see Exod. 4.22; Isa. 49.3). In short, the people Israel, as the Lord's vassal, become prepared to meet him as a result of the Davidic king's mission of forerunner (see 51.7-11; 52.6-15; 55.3-7, etc.). During the series of events that precedes the Lord's coming, Israel, as 'Zion,' may receive protection through divine intervention by proxy, because of the Davidic king's righteousness (see I, **b. A Structural Synthesis**). However, the Lord's universal coming to the earth occurs when vassal Israel (Zion) itself achieves righteousness (see 59.19-60.3, 19-21; 62.1-2, 11-12). Zion's human model of this divine attribute is *righteousness* personified in the Davidic king (see 51.1, 7; 56.1, etc.), a synthesis of the righteous heroes of biblical history.

c. A Covenant Synthesis. The 'new' Covenant in the Book of Isaiah is patterned not after one but all the covenants of biblical history. Basic to the New Covenant is a grant of land and offspring (see 51.2-3; 60.21-22), such as was promised by covenant to Abraham (see Gen. 15.18; 17.2-7). However, the land with which the righteous are endowed is a place protected by the presence of the Lord (see 26.1-4; 30.27-30; 60.18), an ingredient of the Davidic covenant (see I, **b. A Structural Synthesis**). On the other hand, the offspring with which the righteous are blessed are endowed with the Lord's words placed in their mouth (see 51.16; 59.21), a feature of the Levitical covenant (see Mal. 2.4-7). Moreover, the land of the righteous is a land regenerated to a paradisaical glory by a reversal of covenant curses (see 35.1-2; 44.3; 51.3); and the offspring of the righteous are ordained as the priests of the Lord (see 61.6, 9-10; cf. Num. 25.11-13). Different from the Abrahamic, Levitical and Davidic covenants, which were made by the Lord with righteous individuals, the New Covenant is made with the righteous nation Israel, or Zion (see

---

[69] The messianic nature of the above Isaianic metaphors was understood in part by the Qumran community, as has been observed by John V. Chamberlain, 'The Functions of God as Messianic Titles in the Complete Isaiah Scroll,' *VT*, 5 (1955), pp. 366-72.

51.16; 61.8);[70] this corporate dimension is an aspect of the Sinai covenant (see Exod. 24.7-8). Unlike the Sinai covenant, but like the Abrahamic, Levitical and Davidic covenants, is the unconditional nature of the Isaianic Covenant (see 59.21). Its unconditional character appears most prominently in Chapter 54, a chapter in the Book of Isaiah in which are present nearly all elements of the New Covenant: verses 1-3 discuss Zion's offspring and land; verses 4-8 detail the unconditional nature of the Covenant; verses 9-10 include the covenant of Noah among those serving as types for the New Covenant (see Gen. 9.9-11)—the New Covenant is made with those who survive a universal cataclysm of the order of the Flood, in which mountains are removed and hills collapse with quaking; verses 11-12 depict the glorious habitat of the survivors; verse 13 represents the spiritual endowment of their offspring by the Lord; verses 14-17 detail the conditions of divine protection for the righteous. In brief, the New (eschatological) Covenant is a synthesis of all previous covenants of the Lord with individuals and with Israel: an endowment of land protected by the presence of the Lord and offspring endowed with the Spirit of the Lord, made unconditionally with a righteous remnant of Israel after a universal cataclysm of the order of the Flood.

The Davidic king's personification of the *covenant* (see 42.6; 49.8), a term which in that instance serves as a metaphor, denotes that he is its mediator. His mediatory role, as it relates to the Covenant, is that of a lawgiver and *light* to the nations (see 42.4, 6; 49.6) and of a *witness* (Heb. ʿēd, or 'testator'), *prince* (Heb. *nāgîd*, or 'leader') and *lawgiver* (Heb. *mĕṣawwēh*, or 'commander') to the peoples (see 55.3-4). In one respect, the Davidic king's mediatory role differs from that of Moses to Israel only in that the Davidic king's mission is to a people in bondage among the nations (see 42.4-7; 49.5-13; 55.3-13); in another respect, it identifies in a personal way the righteous of Israel with the Davidic king.

[70] Cf. the covenant formula 'my people/your God,' Lev. 26.9, 12.

206

Acknowledgements

This book could never have appeared in this beautiful and useful format without the work of several gifted individuals who, having caught the vision of Isaiah, have generously donated their skills and much time to *The Apocalyptic Book of Isaiah*. Among many who have supported and encouraged me, I owe especial thanks to Arthur Henry King for his unwavering personal encouragement and guidance; Geri Bartholomew, who typed the manuscript; Ester Mortensen, who checked the references in the *Key*; Don Norton, who made editorial suggestions; Rusel K. Hirst, who meticulously reviewed the language of the translation; Lori Schlinker Reynolds, who designed the jacket; Tamara and Thomas K. Hinckley, who designed and typeset the book; a sponsor who generously met the cost of printing; and my wife Cathy.